How To Teach Verbal Behavior

PRO-ED Series on Autism Spectrum Disorders
Edited by Richard L. Simpson

Titles in the Series

HOW TO TEACH
VERBAL BEHAVIOR

Peter Sturmey

An International Publisher

8700 Shoal Creek Boulevard
Austin, Texas 78757-6897
800/897-3202   Fax 800/397-7633
www.proedinc.com

An International Publisher

© 2008 by PRO-ED, Inc.
8700 Shoal Creek Boulevard
Austin, Texas 78757-6897
800/897-3202   Fax 800/397-7633
www.proedinc.com

Library of Congress Cataloging-in-Publication Data

Sturmey, Peter.
    How to teach verbal behavior / Peter Sturmey.
        p. cm. — (PRO-ED series on autism spectrum disorders)
    Includes bibliographical references.
    ISBN-13: 978-1-4164-0147-6 (pbk.)
    1. Autistic children—Education. 2. Verbal behavior. I. Title.
    LC4717.S78 2008
    371.94—dc22
                                                        2007047908

Art Director: Jason Crosier
Designer: Nancy McKinney
This book is designed in Nexus Serif TF and Neutra Text.

Printed in the United States of America

1   2   3   4   5   6   7   8   9   10   17   16   15   14   13   12   11   10   09   08

Contents

About Autism Spectrum Disorders

Autism spectrum disorders (ASD) are complex, neurologically based developmental disabilities that typically appear early in life. The Autism Society of America (2004) estimates that as many as 1.5 million people in the United States have autism or some form of pervasive developmental disorder. Indeed, its prevalence makes ASD an increasingly common and currently the fastest-growing developmental disability. ASD are perplexing and enigmatic. According to the *Diagnostic and Statistical Manual of Mental Disorders*, individuals with ASD have difficulty in interacting normally with others; exhibit speech, language, and communication difficulties (e.g., delayed speech, echolalia); insist on routines and environmental uniformity; engage in self-stimulatory and stereotypic behaviors; and respond atypically to sensory stimuli (American Psychiatric Association, 2000; Simpson & Myles, 1998). In some cases, aggressive and self-injurious behavior may be present in these individuals. Yet, in tandem with these characteristics, children with ASD often have normal patterns of physical growth and development, a wide range of cognitive and language capabilities, and some individuals with ASD have highly developed and unique abilities (Klin, Volkmar, & Sparrow, 2000). These widely varied characteristics necessitate specially designed interventions and strategies orchestrated by knowledgeable and skilled professionals.

Preface to the Series

Teaching and managing learners with ASD can be demanding, but favorable outcomes for children and youth with autism and autism-related disabilities depend on professionals using appropriate and valid methods in their education. Because identifying and correctly using effective teaching methods is often enormously challenging (National Research Council, 2001; Simpson et al., 2005), it is the intent of this series to provide professionals with scientifically based methods for intervention. Each book in the series is designed to assist professionals and parents in choosing and correctly using a variety of interventions that have the potential to produce significant benefits for children and youth with ASD. Written in a user-friendly, straightforward fashion by qualified and experienced professionals, the books are aimed at individuals who seek practical solutions and strategies for successfully working with learners with ASD.

Richard L. Simpson
Series Editor

References

American Psychiatric Association. (2000). *Diagnostic and statistical manual of mental disorders* (4th ed., text rev.). Washington, DC: Author.

Autism Society of America. (2004). *What is autism?* Retrieved March 11, 2005, from http:// autism-society.org

Klin, A., Volkmar, F., & Sparrow, S. (2000). *Asperger syndrome.* New York: Guilford Press.

National Research Council. (2001). *Educating children with autism.* Committee on Educational Interventions for Children with Autism, Division of Behavioral and Social Sciences and Education. Washington, DC: National Academy Press.

Simpson, R., de Boer-Ott, S., Griswold, D., Myles, B., Byrd, S., Ganz, J., et al. (2005). *Autism spectrum disorders: Interventions and treatments for children and youth.* Thousand Oaks, CA: Corwin Press.

Simpson, R. L., & Myles, B. S. (1998). *Educating children and youth with autism: Strategies for effective practice.* Austin, TX: PRO-ED.

Introduction

Verbal Behavior: The Big Picture

Children and adults with autism have tremendous problems communicating with other people. Many do not talk at all. Those that do often have enormous difficulty. Their speech is often limited and difficult for others to respond to. Language is an important part of our behavior. It takes typically developing children many years to master it. Thus, teaching language to children with autism is a daunting task.

The term *verbal behavior* has become fashionable. Some parents and practitioners ask service providers for "verbal behavior" instead of applied behavior analysis (ABA). However, verbal behavior is nothing special. It is just behavior.

The technology of teaching verbal behavior has certainly changed a great deal over the last 10 years. Still, the methods used to teach verbal behavior are all based on the same learning principles as those for teaching any other kind of behavior.

What is verbal behavior?

Verbal behavior is behavior mediated by other people's behavior. It is not the same as speech. Some forms of nonvocal behavior, such as pointing and writing, are verbal behavior. The first section, Verbal Behavior Is Not What You Think It Is, discusses these themes. To teach verbal behavior you must have effective reinforcers. You can reliably identify these reinforcers through paired stimulus preference assessments. The second section, What Does Your Child Like? discusses this. When teaching verbal behavior, you must first check that other people are relevant, reinforcing stimuli. One way to do this is to observe whether a child approaches particular people. If a child does not approach or if he or she avoids some or all people, you must teach this. You must establish a child's good relationships with others by pairing other people with known reinforcers and by removing aversive stimuli. This is covered in the third section, Other People: You Gotta Love 'Em.

Teaching verbal behavior often begins with teaching requests (mands). You should teach reaching for and pointing to highly preferred stimuli and teach mands to terminate aversive stimuli. Good mand teaching involves using *reinforcer deprivation* prior to training. Finally, you should shape progressively more sophisticated forms of mands. After your child has learned to point, teach vocal approximations, words, and word combinations. The section Ask Nicely! discusses these themes.

Teaching verbal behavior also involves teaching *generalized imitation.* It also involves teaching using *imitative prompts* and *fading.* This is covered in the section titled Watching Other People. Following this, the section titled Say Something! Anything! focuses on expanding simple mands, from requests for food using single words to using grammatically complex sentences, in addition to information mands and chains of mands. The seventh section, What's That?, and the eighth section, "The Wheels on the Bus Go . . ." focus on teaching advanced mands, receptive language, teaching other aspects of language, the unique language and verbal features and functions of objects and people, textual responses, and varied verbal behavior. These sections also discuss teaching nonverbal forms of language, using children's unique interests to teach verbal behavior, and how to promote generalization. The final section, Last Words on Verbal Behavior, discusses how to promote variability in language, as well as practical issues such as getting educated about verbal behavior and recruiting a well-trained staff. This final section closes with a list of further readings, Internet resources, and organizations you will find helpful. Appendixes A, B, C, D, and E are reproducible forms.

Acknowledgments

I should like to thank my friend and colleague Emerita Professor Claire L. Poulson for teaching me so much about language, applied behavior analysis, and autism. Thank you to Adrienne Fitzer, who has co-edited two books with me, one specifically on this topic. I would also like to thank my graduate students who have worked with me on research related to language and autism, including Dr. Randi Sarakoff, Dr. Ron Lee, Dr. Mari Watanabe-Rose, Michael Lafasakis, Ben Thomas, Haven Bernstein, Darlene Nigro, Lori Finn, Nancy Dib, Tommy Gianoumis, Laura Sieverling, and John Ward-Horner.

Verbal Behavior Is Not What You Think It Is

OBJECTIVES

In this section, you will learn to:

1. Define verbal behavior;
2. Define and give examples of Skinner's four basic verbal operants—the mand, tact, echoic, and intraverbal;
3. Define and give examples of speaker and listener behavior;
4. Describe the implications for teaching language to children with ASD; and
5. Describe the importance of generalization and verbal behavior.

Mike and Jamal: Who Can Talk?

"This is the news from Channel 11 coming to you from Cleveland...." Mike says many words every minute. He has no verbal behavior. All he does is repeat things he heard from the TV. He is uninterested in other people. He does look at the TV for hours if not pulled away. He has not learned that people can do things for you. He has not learned that they deliver reinforcers. He has not learned that interacting with people can be fun. The only reinforcer maintaining his words is the sound of the words themselves.

On the other hand, Jamal has excellent verbal behavior. He just does not speak—yet. Jamal points and even throws tantrums to get the things he likes. He drags his mom to things that he wants but cannot reach. He has learned that his family members give him the toys and snacks when he looks at these things. Jamal has learned that other people are interesting. Soon, Jamal's family will teach him how to make sounds for things he likes. Eventually, they will teach him to ask for things with words. Over time, Jamal will not need to point or throw tantrums for those things.

Professor Fred Skinner's Theory of Verbal Behavior

Burrhus Frederic (B.F.) Skinner is famous for his research and theories o
learning. He was always interested in the application of learning to people
His research was the basis of applied behavior analysis, though he did littl
applied work himself. Rather, he worked behind the scenes to make it hap
pen. He trained many of the researchers who went on to do the importan
research in the 1960s that children with autism all benefit from today.

In 1957, Skinner recalled that during a formal dinner in 1934 [Profes
sor] Alfred North Whitehead had "agreed that science might be successful iı
accounting for human behavior provided one made an exception of verba
behavior. Here, he [Whitehead] insisted something else must be at work. . .
'Let me see you,' he said, 'account for my behavior as I sit here saying, "Nı
black scorpion is falling on this table."' The next morning I [Skinner] drev
up the outline of the present study" (Skinner, 1957, p. 457).

It took Skinner 23 years from that dinner before he published his bool
Verbal Behavior. It took behaviorists another 30 years before we really startec
to grasp the ideas in this book. Only over the last 10 years has applied worl
on verbal behavior and autism taken off.

So, What Is Verbal Behavior?

Skinner defined *verbal behavior* as "behavior mediated by other people." *Me
diated* means that another person is in the middle of delivering reinforce
ment. When behavior is directly reinforced—for example, when one presses
buttons on a remote control to turn on the TV—that is an example of non
verbal behavior. However, when another person delivers the reinforcer tha
reinforces the verbal behavior—for example, when someone hands some
one else the remote control that he or she asked for—that is an example
of verbal behavior. Here is another example. If your child reaches for a fa
vorite puzzle and picks it up, that is not verbal behavior. If your child says
"Elephant puzzle, please," and you hand your child the elephant puzzle, ther
that is verbal behavior. If your child drags you by your arm to the elephan
puzzle and cries until you give it to him or her, that, too, is verbal behav
ior. So, if your child asks, cries, signs, sings, hands over a Picture Exchange
Communication System (PECS) (Pyramid Educational Consultants, 2008)
symbol, writes you a note, jumps up and down until you give him or her the
puzzle—and you do—all of these are examples of verbal behavior.

Four Common Verbal Operants

Skinner proposed that verbal behavior is operant behavior. That is, it operates on the environment to obtain reinforcers. Skinner identified four common verbal operants: mand, tact, echoic, and intraverbal. Characteristic antecedent stimuli ("triggers") and reinforcers ("rewards") define each of the operants.

1. *Mand.* In everyday language, think of a mand as a request. In technical terms, the antecedent stimuli that control mands are *reinforcer deprivation* or *aversive stimulation*. The mand often describes its own reinforcers. For example, the request "doll" is affected by deprivation of a play doll. Suppose a child has not played with her favorite baby doll for a couple of days. She will now very likely ask for her doll a lot. Asking for her doll is reinforced when the listener gives the speaker the doll.

2. *Tact.* In everyday language, think of a tact as naming, labeling, and commenting. A tact is controlled by a previous nonverbal stimulus. It is reinforced by the listener's interaction. For example, suppose a person says, "Looks like rain," after the clouds get dark. Then a second person says, "Sure does." The first speaker's verbal behavior is a tact, because it is controlled by a nonverbal stimulus—the dark clouds. It is also a tact because the other person's interaction reinforced it.

3. *Echoic.* In everyday language, think of an echoic response as an imitation. An echoic is controlled by the other person's verbal model. It matches what the other person said *exactly*. It is also controlled by some generalized reinforcer, such as praise from the other person. For example, the preacher says, "Hallelujah," and the crowd also says, "Hallelujah." Then the preacher says, "Amen!" The preacher's first "Hallelujah" is the model. The crowd's response matches the model exactly. Thus it is an echoic. The "Amen" is the reinforcer for the crowd's having emitted "Hallelujah." Generalized imitation and echoic prompts are common examples of echoics.

4. *Intraverbal.* In everyday language, think of an intraverbal as answering questions. An intraverbal is evoked by another person's verbal behavior. It does not exactly match it. Examples include answering questions, or filling in the gap in a song that someone else starts. Much conversation and many intellectual verbal skills are intraverbals.

Speaker and Listener

Skinner made a distinction between the speaker and the listener. The speaker emits verbal behavior. The listener delivers the reinforcer that maintains the speaker's verbal behavior. The speaker's job is to influence the listener's behavior effectively to deliver reinforcers. The listener's job is to cue the speaker effectively as to which responses are appropriate. The listener also must accurately discriminate the speaker's verbal behavior. Finally, the listener must reinforce the speaker's behavior effectively. During conversation, each person may switch roles as speaker and listener.

COREY AS SPEAKER:	Hi! [Mands for attention].
JERRIE AS LISTENER:	What's up? [Reinforces "Hi" with attention. Cues Corey to speak.]
JERRIE AS SPEAKER:	Cool shirt! [Emits an intraverbal. Tacts an object.]
COREY AS LISTENER:	Just back from Hawaii. [Reinforces tact with attention. Also functions as an intraverbal.]
COREY AS SPEAKER:	I got pics. [Intraverbal related to the stimulus "Hawaii." Tacts objects. Mands for attention.]
JERRIE AS LISTENER:	Hawaii! [Delayed echoic] Later, Dude! [Intraverbal related to "pics." Also the pictures may have been an aversive stimulus. Jerrie mands for escape from pictures.]
COREY AS SPEAKER:	Later, then. [Reinforces escape mand. Also functions as mand to terminate the conversation.]
JERRIE AS LISTENER:	Later. [Reinforces escape mand. Also functions as mand to terminate conversation.]

In the weird world of verbal behavior, one person can be both the speaker and the listener. Much of our thinking with words involves switching roles as speaker and listener. We are the speaker when we mand to ourselves, "Get the pen." We are the listener when we obtain the reinforcer pick up the pen, and tell ourselves, "OK." Instantly, we are again the speaker when we say, "It's the wrong one," tacting the object and manding for a different pen.

Verbal Behavior and People with Autism

Skinner's (1957) analysis of verbal behavior has at least six implications for teaching language to people with autism.

1. You have to teach each verbal operant separately. Saying "Chip" might be a mand, a tact, an echoic, or an intraverbal. Learning to mand by saying "Chip" is no guarantee that your child can label a chip.

2. If your child works for a range of reinforcers, you can probably teach mands relatively easily. This is because you can control the delivery of a powerful reinforcer.

3. The problem comes with the other verbal operants that are reinforced by attention. Many children with autism are indifferent to others. Some even find other people aversive. To teach tacts and intraverbals, you have to make other people reinforcing. Until you do that, you cannot teach tacts and intraverbals.

4. The reinforcer that maintains echoics is the match between what the model says and the learner's response. It takes a lot of careful teaching to establish this as a reinforcer.

5. If your child does not speak yet, there is still a lot you can do. Identify and teach more mature forms of verbal behavior. Observe how your child approaches and avoids things. See if your child leads you to things he or she wants, throws tantrums for reinforcers, or shows other maladaptive behavior to "ask" for something. Figure out how to teach him or her a better way to ask. Maybe you can teach your child to point or to make a sound like the word.

6. Skinner's distinction of speaker and listener is very important. To teach language, there must be both an effective speaker *and* an effective listener. The person doing the teaching is a listener. The listener has to be a responsive and effective communication partner. He or she has to present the right antecedent and deliver the right reinforcer. To be an effective communicator, your child must be both an effective speaker *and* an effective listener. He or she has to be able to present the right cues to another person and to deliver the right reinforcer to the communication partner.

Generalization and Verbal Behavior

Typically, we assume that language and communication skills are something locked inside our heads. Traditional language therapy consists of somehow stimulating the brain to acquire language. Once language is there, the person is supposed to carry language around with them at all times. Thus, many traditional approaches to language merely build vocabulary or teach grammar. These approaches usually fail. They fail because they do not teach the four previously discussed verbal operants. They fail because they do not teach *how* to use words.

Applied behavior analysis assumes that verbal behavior is just like any other behavior. It depends on the environment. Individuals may show verbal behavior in some situations and not in others. They may show verbal behavior with some people but not with others. Therefore, we should carefully analyze and assess verbal behavior and its use from the start. Probing for generalization after training is a mistake.

An example of a generalization plan is shown in the example below.

From Real Life
Teaching Helen to "Hang" with Different People in Different Places

Helen seemed to do well in her classroom for students with autism. She answered questions correctly, she talked about things in pictures, and she completed math and English language worksheets independently. In her mainstream class, however, she was very different from her typically developing peers. Helen sat at the back of the classroom with her aides. She said nothing. Her body rocked. Her peers whispered to each other, made mean comments about each other's belongings, and asked for pencils. Some students even answered the teacher's questions. Despite her excellent language in the autism class, Helen showed almost no verbal behavior in her mainstream classroom.

This was a generalization problem. She spoke in her autism class. She did not speak in her mainstream class. She spoke with her classroom staff. She did not speak with her typical peers. She needed a program to promote generalization.

We began by teaching Helen to have a simple conversation. We used scripts and script fading. We identified a very simple conversation that should be interesting to her peers. It had four parts: "What's up?," "What did you do last night?," "I watched TV," "Bye!" At first she read the sentences to her aides from cards. These aides made a variety of responses to Helen. Once Helen had learned this skill, we faded the scripts by cutting off parts of the cards little by little. We programmed generalization by having a conversation in different parts of the room, while sitting and standing, and with different people. After only 90 minutes, Helen had simple conversations with a typically developing peer in the autism classroom.

Now we were ready to teach Helen to talk to her peers in the mainstream classroom!

SUMMARY

This section introduced basic principles, concepts, and information linked to verbal behavior. It discussed how to instruct learners with autism to use verbal behavior. Important elements of this section are summarized below.

1. Verbal behavior is behavior mediated by other people.
2. Verbal behavior is operant behavior.
3. The four main verbal operants connected to verbal behavior are mands, tacts, echoics, and intraverbals. They are each defined by their own characteristic antecedent and reinforcer.
4. During verbal behavior, there is a speaker who emits verbal behavior and a listener who cues and reinforces appropriate verbal behavior.
5. You must teach your child each verbal operant separately.
6. You must teach your child both speaker and listener behavior.
7. Verbal behavior depends on special reinforcers, such as attention from other people. So children must learn that attention is a reinforcer.

What Does Your Child Like?

OBJECTIVES

In this section, you will learn to:

1. Define reinforcer;
2. Systematically identify reinforcers;
3. Recognize factors that influence the power of reinforcers; and
4. Build some simple programs to teach your child verbal behavior based around preference assessments and your child's approach and avoidance behavior.

What Is a Reinforcer?

A first step in teaching your child verbal behavior is to identify reinforcers. In everyday language, think of reinforcers as "rewards." A more technical definition of a reinforcer is a consequence that increases the future probability of a behavior. That is, a stimulus is only a reinforcer if it happens *after* the behavior *and* if it increases the behavior in the future. If it does not increase the behavior, it is not a reinforcer. There are many other ways to increase a behavior. Prompts increase a behavior. However, these are different from reinforcers. Prompts occur *before* the target behavior. Drugs, such as caffeine, may also increase a behavior. For example, drinking caffeinated coffee may increase a particular response, such as talking a lot. However, since drinking coffee occurs *before* the desired behavior, it is not a reinforcer. Reinforcers always *follow* a desired behavior.

Reinforcer deprivation also increases behaviors. For example, if an individual is reinforcer deprived, then behavior related to that reinforcer will increase. What happens if nothing has reinforced our behavior for a long time? We start looking around for something interesting.

People all work for different kinds of reinforcers. We work hard to gain access to certain things, such as the money to buy an item we desire. We call these things *positive reinforcers*. We also work hard to remove

11

unpleasant things. These unpleasant things are called *negative reinforcers*. Fo example, a teenager may clean her room to stop her parents' nagging. Som things seem to be naturally reinforcing. For example, it is easy to recogniz the rewarding value of food and oxygen. These are called *primary reinforcer* Other things are acquired tastes. Gold stars, praise, jalapeño peppers, an people are learned reinforcers. These are called *secondary reinforcers*.

Why Should You Assess Your Child's Reinforcers Systematically?

It is important to identify reinforcers accurately. When you use effectiv reinforcers, you can teach your child more effectively. Your child will lear faster and will be more interested in learning. Here are some things you ca do with effective reinforcers and verbal behavior:

- Reinforce a correct response. This will make it more likely that your child will make a correct response in the future.
- Teach your child to ask for things he or she wants.
- Select and use materials that your child finds interesting.
- Choose things that your child likes to talk about.
- Make and use new reinforcers (e.g., tokens and points). Tokens and points are easy to deliver and can be exchanged for desired items later.
- Increase your child's interest in other people.

Identify Your Child's Reinforcers

Research has shown that when you ask people who know a child really wel to identify reinforcers, they are sometimes right and sometimes wrong This is true for family members and for professionals. Thus, there are goo reasons to assess reinforcers systematically. Four ways to do this follow.

Use Reinforcer Checklists

Completing a reinforcer checklist is a good place to start to help identif your child's reinforcers. You can find an example of a completed Reinforce Assessment Form in Figure 1. A blank form is in Appendix A. When yo have completed the form, write out your child's list of probable reinforcers

Child's Name: __Juan Martello__

Date: __Friday, May 25, 2007__

Possible reinforcer	Examples
Foods, such as snacks and candies	Chocolate-chip cookies Cake M&Ms Goldfish crackers
Drinks, such as sips of Coke	None
Toys, such as dolls and trains	His animal book His computer spelling game
Activities, such as jumping on a trampoline	Adults swinging him around Running Playing on the swing
Places, such as a favorite chair	None
People, such as a favorite teacher assistant	None
Secondary reinforcers, such as points, money, tokens	None
Items or topics he or she likes to obsess on	None
Things he or she likes to avoid or quit, such as crowded places	Noisy people Jamie, because she screams near him
Anything else he or she likes	Loves playing with water

List the five most probable reinforcers. (List the very best one first, then the second best one, and so on.)

1. Playing with water

2. Any sweet thing to eat

3. Adults swinging him around

4. Playing on the swing

5. Animal book

FIGURE 1. Completed Reinforcer Assessment Form for Juan, a 9-year-old boy with pervasive developmental disabilities.

Observe Approach and Avoidance Behavior

Another easy way to identify possible reinforcers is to observe your child closely. Look for things your child approaches and avoids. Your child can approach things and people in three ways. These include (a) using words or sounds to ask for things, such as saying, "j" for juice; (b) looking, reaching, and grabbing at things or people, such as pointing to a cup of juice; and (c) turning his or her body toward things or people, such as turning around to look at a cup of juice.

Your child can also avoid things and people in three ways. These include (a) using words or sounds to remove or avoid things, such as saying, "No"; (b) pushing things and people away and throwing and dropping things, such as pushing a pencil and paper off the desk; and (c) turning his or her body away from things or people, such as turning away from the table when asked to work. Figure 2 provides an example of a form that you can use to record the things your child approaches or avoids. You can find a blank copy in Appendix B. It also can be useful to record *how* your child approaches and avoids things and people.

Do Preference Assessments with Objects

Preference assessments are systematic ways to identify your child's reinforcers. There are many ways to do preference assessments. One efficient method is called *multiple stimulus preference assessment without replacement.* Here are the six steps.

1. Place seven items on a tray in front of your child.
2. Write down which item your child selects.
3. Remove the tray. Wait for your child to interact with the item for 5 seconds. Then remove the item. (If it is a food item, wait until your child has finished eating the item.)
4. Change the places of all the items on the tray.
5. Present the tray again. Repeat steps 2 through 4.
6. Continue until your child selects all the items or your child stops taking any items.

This approach is quick and easy. For example, before you teach, grab a few toys and snacks. Do the preference assessment. Then teach using the child's preferred items. For example, suppose you want to teach your child to ask for things. First, conduct a preference assessment. During the assessment, look carefully at your child's behavior to see how he or she asks for things. This could include pointing, reaching, making sounds, or using words or phrases. Use the preferred stimuli to prompt your child to request. Put them in plain sight, but out of reach. Wait for him or her to ask nicely.

Child's Name: _Juan Martello_

Date: _Friday, May 25, 2007_

Time	Approach Verbal (V) Hands (H) Body (B)	Avoid Verbal (V) Hands (H) Body (B)	Object or person approached or avoided
09:31	H		Pointed to toy car
09:31	H + V		Pointed to toy car and cried
09:32		H	Pushed teaching materials away
09:32		B + V	Turned away and cried when asked to work
09:33	H		Pointed to blocks
09:33	V		Said, "Ca" for car

FIGURE 2. Completed Approach and Avoidance Form for Juan, a 9-year-old boy with pervasive developmental disabilities.

Only then give the child the requested item. Figure 3 is an example of a completed Preference Assessment Form. Use the blank form in Appendix C to record the preference assessment with your own child. Later you will see how to use this information.

Do Preference Assessments with Photographs and Words

Using photographs instead of actual objects can be convenient since you do not have to present the actual objects. You can also present things such as movies and places to visit that are easy to present using pictures. You can present photographs on a tray, just as with actual objects. You can also systematically present pairs of photographs for the child to indicate his or her preference.

Another way to assess possible reinforcers is to use words. You can do this with a child who has good language skills. Simply ask, "What do you like: cookies or a book?" and go through all the combinations of items.

Child's Name: Juan Martello

Date: Friday, May 25, 2007

Item	Order selected
1. Glass of water	1
2. M&Ms	2
3. Animal book	7
4. Goldfish crackers	4
5. Small piece of cookie	5
6. Cheese doodle	6
7. Small piece of chocolate	3

FIGURE 3. Completed Preference Assessment Form for Juan, a 9-year-old boy with pervasive developmental disabilities.

Preference assessments using photos and words are convenient, bu these methods can be time-consuming. Also, your child must have goo cognitive skills to participate in these kinds of preference assessments. Fig ure 4 is an example of a completed paired stimulus reinforcer assessmen using this format. Use the blank form in Appendix D to conduct a paired stimulus preference assessment with your child.

But Is It a Reinforcer?

Preference assessments do not directly assess whether or not the choser stimuli work as reinforcers. The only way you can figure out if preferred stimuli are really reinforcers is to use them while you are teaching. Once you have identified a couple of highly preferred stimuli, test them by using them to teach something useful and important. Select a goal in your child's current program. Then see if he or she can learn when working for a pre ferred stimulus.

	B Video	C McDonald's	D Pizza Hut	E Swimming
A Bike	A	A	A	A
B Video		B	D	E
C McDonald's			D	E
D Pizza Hut				D

Summary of choices

Item	Tally
A - Bike	4
B - Video	1
C - McDonald's	0
D - Pizza Hut	3
E - Swimming	2

FIGURE 4. Completed Paired Stimulus Preference Assessment Form. *Note.* From these results, we can see a preference for riding a bike and no interest in going to McDonald's. Thus, one should incorporate the bike and related activities and stimuli into this child's program.

Reinforcer Deprivation and Satiation

The power of a stimulus to reinforce behavior depends on reinforcer deprivation and satiation. *Deprivation* refers to a recent period of time during which the reinforcer is unavailable. *Satiation* refers to a recent period of time in which the reinforcer was presented a great deal. Reinforcer deprivation has at least two effects on behavior. First, it increases the power of the stimulus as a reinforcer for a while. Second, it increases other behaviors that a reinforcer has previously increased. For example, suppose it is hot outside and you have not drunk water for a while. Under these conditions you will walk further and pay more for a drink if you have to. Also, you will look around for something to drink, go to places where you have previously gotten drinks, and will talk about drinks. Reinforcer satiation has the opposite effects on behavior. What do we do after spending hours with crowds of talkative people? We go to our room, close the door, and turn the phone off. If someone comes to talk to us, we turn away and ask them to give us some peace and quiet.

Task Effort and Difficulty

The power of a stimulus to be a reinforcer also depends on task effort and difficulty. You might chase a $20 bill down the street for a long time. However, you might not bother to pick up a penny off the floor. If a penny is right in front of you near your hand, you might put it in your pocket. If you see a penny across the room, you might not even give it a second glance. These two factors—how much we have recently experienced the reinforcer and how difficult the task is—change the value of a stimulus as a reinforcer from moment to moment. So, you should not expect even a highly preferred stimulus to *always* be effective. Even a highly preferred stimulus will be much less effective after satiation. This would be especially true when asked to complete a difficult task. For example, would you work hard for 5 minutes of TV time after you have watched TV for hours? Probably not.

You can use reinforcer deprivation during teaching. For example, suppose you do a preference assessment first thing in the morning. Now, also suppose this preference assessment identifies a set of reinforcer pictures that are moderately preferred. You can put the pictures away in the closet for 4 hours. After lunch, your child will be satiated to foods. This is now a good time to teach language skills using the preferred pictures.

The following scenario illustrates common challenges and program issues related to reinforcer assessment and use of reinforcers.

From Real Life
"My Child Got Bored with ABA."

Recently, I heard a dad say, "My child got bored with ABA." My reaction was, "It must have been really bad ABA." If ABA is done well, your child will look forward to learning. Your child will run to the place where he or she learned in the past, smile, reach for the teaching materials, and look eager to learn.

Something was badly wrong with the use of reinforcement in the program. Maybe the so-called reinforcers that were used were not reinforcers at all. Maybe the instructor had not used reinforcers correctly. For example, perhaps the instructor did not deliver them immediately or asked for too much behavior for too little reinforcement. Sadly, the family withdrew their child from the ABA program that could have helped their child a lot.

What Does Juan Like?

Look back at Figures 1, 2, and 3, which contain our preference assessments with Juan. We have already learned a lot. He loves water. He likes sweet things, such as cookies, cake, and M&Ms. He also likes Goldfish crackers, his animal book, a toy car, blocks, and a computer spelling game. He avoids noisy people (especially Jamie) and work, at least when there are more interesting cars and blocks around. We have also learned that he has some good verbal behavior. He points a lot, says, "Ca" for car, and pushes things away that he does not like. We have lots to work with!

We can build on these positive elements to teach him to request things he really likes. We can start by using pointing as a general way to request. If he says, "Ca" for car, maybe we can teach him to say, "Bu" for books. Perhaps he has other sounds we could use to teach him more words. So far, we have seen only one way to communicate that he does not like something: pushing the thing away. This is a problem. We have to teach him a better way to say "No." Perhaps we can teach him to hold up his hand. It might be a good idea to put favorite toys and blocks out of the way when we teach him. Instead, we can use them to teach requesting during play after a teaching session.

SUMMARY

This section discussed basic information on using reinforcement and reinforcers to teach verbal behavior. Here are four points to remember.

1. A reinforcer is a consequence that increases the future probability of behavior. There are a variety of reinforcers. These include positive and negative reinforcers. There are also primary and secondary reinforcers.

2. You can identify possible reinforcers using three methods:
   (a) Reinforcer checklists,
   (b) Observations of a child's approach and avoidance behavior, and
   (c) Preference assessments. (If you are going to conduct a preference assessment, use a *multiple stimulus preference without replacement assessment.*)

3. Many factors affect power and effectiveness of reinforcers. These include reinforcer satiation and deprivation, as well as task effort and difficulty. Use reinforcer deprivation to make your teaching more effective. Be aware of reinforcer satiation. Avoid teaching with ineffective reinforcers.

4. When you conduct preference assessments, use the information to build an effective communication program for your child. Do this by using the preferred stimuli as part of his or her program. You can also build on current communication skills and preferences to extend your child's language.

Other People: You Gotta Love 'Em!

OBJECTIVES

In this section, you will learn to:

1. Describe why building relationships is important for teaching verbal behavior;
2. Recognize how people become generalized conditioned reinforcers; and
3. Effectively build relationships with children who have autism.

Marie and Stephan

Marie had made a lot of progress during discrete trials teaching. She had learned to sit with her hands down for 10 minutes and to imitate her teacher's gross motor behaviors, such as clapping and raising her hands. When her teacher reinforced correct responses with edibles, she worked well. She was, however, still quite indifferent to other people. Marie's parents and therapist had a big job ahead of them. Marie had to learn to work for praise alone and to recognize that other people were interesting.

Stephan was a cute, 9-year-old boy with autism. He had an advanced vocabulary—better than that of his peers with typical development. If you needed to know the definition of *neutrophils* or *eosinophils*, Stephan was your man! However, talking to people was very hard for Stephan. He could start a conversation, and he often said some quite sophisticated grammatical sentences. But sometimes his mom had to cue him to start talking. Often, after a few sentences, he would find the texture of a concrete wall more interesting than talking to a person. One of Stephan's problems was that people were not powerful reinforcers for talking.

21

Why Liking Other People Is Essential to Verbal Behavior

In the opening section, Verbal Behavior Is Not What You Think It Is, we learned that verbal behavior is operant behavior. The reinforcers that follow a verbal behavior greatly affect its future occurrence. *Mands* specify their own reinforcer. For example, suppose a child points at a swing and then often uses the swing. The swing is probably the reinforcer maintaining the pointing mand for swing. *Tacts, echoics,* and *intraverbals* are not like mands. Attention from other people—not things or snacks—reinforce tacts, echoics, and intraverbals. So, if attention from others is not reinforcing, you cannot teach them these three verbal operants. Therefore, you must first establish attention from other people as a reinforcer.

Many young children with autism are indifferent to other people. Some even find others aversive and work to avoid others. Another more subtle problem is that some children with autism have highly individual interests that are powerful reinforcers and that compete with attention, if attention is a weak reinforcer. For example, suppose your child loves vacuum cleaners. Your child may find that reviewing a vacuum cleaner's parts is more interesting and reinforcing than talking with or even looking at another person.

Look back at the two children we discussed earlier in this section. Marie has the first problem. For Marie, other people are not reinforcers. Stephan, on the other hand, has some of both problems. Other people are weak reinforcers *and* competing interests make talking less likely. Both of these children will benefit from learning to make other people conditioned reinforcers. This will then help them learn tacts, echoics, and intraverbals.

Conditioned Reinforcers

Definition

Recall that certain stimuli (e.g., warmth) are natural, unlearned reinforcers. Other stimuli (e.g., jalapeño peppers) are acquired tastes. We learn that some things become reinforcers. Attention is a powerful reinforcer for most people. Unfortunately, attention is not a powerful reinforcer for many children and youth with autism. Most people have suffered from periods of loneliness, so it is tempting to think that attention is a natural reinforcer. However, when we look at children with autism, we can easily see that attention is not a reinforcer for many of them. So the important task we must do is to establish attention from other people as a reinforcer.

Developing Conditioned Reinforcers

There are many examples of how neutral stimuli become powerful reinforcers. Think how hard we all work for money! But what happens if you give a 3-month-old infant a check? The child would probably drop it on the floor. Most adults would not do that! Why? How did paper become such a powerful reinforcer? By being paired with primary reinforcers many times, money eventually became a secondary reinforcer. We have learned that we can exchange money for snacks, drinks, and warm clothes, especially when we are hungry, thirsty, and cold. We have also learned that money can be exchanged for other secondary reinforcers, such as movie tickets and DVDs. What is especially powerful about money is that you can exchange it for other reinforcers at the right time. When you are hungry, money gets you food. When you are thirsty, money gets you drink. When you are bored, you can buy an interesting book. Money is so much more flexible and convenient than food as a reinforcer. Try talking to your lunch when you are lonely, or eating your phone when you are hungry!

Let us take a look at how we develop *generalized conditioned reinforcers*. A generalized conditioned reinforcer is a secondary reinforcer that has been paired with many different primary and secondary reinforcers. This process can be used as a model for developing people into secondary reinforcers.

We develop conditioned reinforcers by *repeated stimulus pairings*. To establish a token as a reinforcer, a teacher initially gives a child free tokens. The teacher then physically prompts the child to hand over a token. Immediately, the teacher gives the child a primary reinforcer. This is done many times. The teacher then fades the prompt by manually prompting less and less. At the end of this procedure, the child will learn to exchange tokens independently. The tokens reinforce handing the token to another person, storing tokens, and waiting. The teacher teaches waiting by gradually increasing time between giving the tokens and exchanging them. The teacher teaches storing tokens by teaching the child to place the tokens somewhere convenient and safe.

When the child has learned to take and store tokens, and to exchange them, we are ready to use them. We select a very easy task, like putting a block in a box. We gave the child lots of opportunities to earn tokens. If the child has good comprehension, we can instruct him or her about the procedure. Over time, we can begin using the tokens to reinforce many different behaviors. We can also gradually delay token exchange to convenient times, such as break times and the end of the day.

Naturally Occurring Relationship Building

Babies quickly learn that other people deliver reinforcers. They learn that other people deliver milk when they are hungry and something to drink when they are thirsty. When they are cold, other people cuddle them and bring blankets. Other people are repeatedly paired with food when they are hungry, drink when they are thirsty, and warmth when they are cold. Babies also learn that other people remove aversive stimuli. When they are hot, other people take off their clothes and cool them down. When they are sick, other people pick them up and comfort them. Other people are repeatedly paired with relief from aversive stimuli.

In typically developing children, the repeated pairing of other people with positive and negative reinforcers establishes attention from other people as a generalized conditioned reinforcer. This is a naturally occurring process with typically developing children. However, with many children who have autism, this connection often needs to be taught systematically.

Relationship Building Is Hard

Establishing other people as generalized conditioned reinforcers with children who have autism is tough—much harder than token training. Children have no learning history with tokens or points. Unfortunately, many children with autism have learned over the course of years that people are irrelevant or aversive stimuli. Other people have repeatedly presented requests to do things the child does not enjoy, disrupted the child's interesting activities, and even nagged, yelled, and screamed at the child. Since other people have been such aversive stimuli, many children with autism have learned a number of ways to avoid and escape them. They may learn to be passive, to not respond when others approach them, to quietly turn away, and even to throw a tantrum. Your child may have learned that other things are much more interesting than people are. He or she may have learned to engage in repetitive behaviors, such as finger manipulation, head weaving, or object tapping. Relationship building is often an uphill battle because you are working against a lifetime of learning. The From Real Life example that follows illustrates these problems.

From Real Life
The Aversive Behaviorist

I was talking to an ABA therapist who calmly told me that Ryan, a child she worked with, was learning well. However, every time she knocked on the family's front door, the parent would open the door, and the child would look at her, scream, and run away. She had no idea why little Ryan did this. She wondered if the child needed an assessment for his screaming. I never had the heart to tell her the real reason.

What had gone wrong here? The therapist had failed to establish herself as a secondary reinforcer. She had not paired herself with enough known reinforcers, such as fun tasks, and had repeatedly paired herself with too many difficult tasks. Maybe Ryan had learned to work hard and fast to remove the aversive behaviorist.

What To Do

Two steps are the foundation for establishing better relationships between children with autism and other people. First, pair people with known primary and secondary reinforcers. Second, remove all aversive stimuli paired with people.

Pair Yourself with Reinforcers

The second section, What Does Your Child Like?, described four methods to identify potential reinforcers. Pair yourself with these reinforcers as frequently as possible. If your child likes orange juice, then frequently give your child sips of orange juice. If your child likes going to the corner of the room, be the person who takes him or her there. When pairing yourself with reinforcers, follow these rules. First, deliver the reinforcer immediately. *Immediately* means no longer than 2 seconds after the behavior. Do not say, "Wait" or "In a minute." Second, make any child response for the reinforcer extremely easy. Ask very little of your child at the beginning. If your child reaches for you, reinforce that behavior. If your child walks toward you or holds out a hand, reinforce that, too. Identify all aspects of your attention that should reinforce your child's behavior. These include your voice, your smile, and your touch. Here are some of the different kinds of attention you may deliver to your child: your soft voice, tickles, swinging your child up in the air, giving a gentle hug, wrestling your child to the ground, gently stroking your child's face, vigorously patting a child on the back, singing with your child, and picking your child up and throwing him or her up in the air. In the long run, you should make sure that all of these forms of attention will be reinforcers. Thus, you should pair many different kinds of attention with known reinforcers.

Be Responsive to Approach Behavior

Follow your child's lead. Be aware of your child's ways of approaching things and people. Does your child reach, look, hover around, or throw tantrums for items? These are important communication skills. These behaviors tell you what reinforcers to deliver. Information from behavior problems can also be helpful. Suppose that your child often runs to the corner of a room to flick his fingers on plastic toys with hard surfaces. That information may provide ideas about possible reinforcers. Try handing him the toy with hard plastic surfaces a few times. See if he or she starts approaching you. If your child wants to go to a swing, go with him or her. Respond to your child's mands. That is, if the child points to a toy, quickly give him or her the toy. The next example shows the importance of accurately identifying the reinforcer maintaining approaching people.

From Real Life
Professor Sturmey Is Fooled Again

I was working with an 8-year-old boy who had autism. Silently, I was congratulating myself on my relationship-building skills. The child was reaching out to me and stroking my face. What a skilled behaviorist I was!

A staff member burst my bubble. "He likes stimming on your beard," the staff member said.

I suppose if we put some fur on a cup, he would have been as interested in the cup as he was with me.

Avoid Pairing with Aversive Stimuli

In the early stages of building rapport, do not pair yourself with anything unpleasant. Do not make requests. Do not teach. Do not interrupt your child's ongoing behavior. Do not reprimand. If there are unpleasant medical or physical therapy procedures, do not be involved with them. If some of these things must be done, then get someone else who already has good rapport with your child to do them.

Program Generalization Across People

Generalization is an essential part of any ABA program. You must consider generalization at the beginning of any program— not at the end. The same holds true for building relationships. Your long-term goal is for your child to have good relationships with many people. So, identify all the important people in your child's life. These include family members and staff who work with your child. It also includes any neighbors and friends, school staff, and so on. Ensure that each of them has a good relationship with your child.

Children react differently to different people. Look closely at which people your child approaches. Look closely at which people your child avoids. If a child consistently avoids particular people, it is important to attempt to identify and modify the problem. If you have family members or staff who often are associated with child avoidance behavior, you have a problem. Your child will not work well with those people. He or she may even learn to show behavior problems with them. Take a careful look at those people that your child avoids. Look at the activities your child does with staff members. Look at how the adults respond to your child's behavior. Figure out what is going wrong. Ensure that these people stop pairing themselves with aversive stimuli. Ensure that they do not engage in behaviors that irritate your child, such as interrupting them or pulling them away from things your child likes. Make sure they pair themselves with fun things. The following From Real Life example illustrates how a smart program director had everything figured out when it came to building good relationships among their new staff and their students with autism.

From Real Life
Learning to Get Along from the Beginning

Dr. Schneider directed a small ABA school for children with autism. Staff turnover could sometimes be high. Training new staff was something she had to do every month.

Dr. Schneider knew that many of her students had a lot of problems getting along with new staff members. She knew that building good relationships from the start was essential if the children were to respond well to the staff. So, she had a special program for new employees. During their first week, new staff did not teach. Their only job was to have fun with the kids. They could hand out snacks, play chase, hand out tokens, exchange tokens, tickle the children who liked that, and hang out with the kids. They could observe programs being run. They could read the children's program books, of course. But new staff did not get involved in anything unpleasant, like a physical therapy program or an activity the child did not like. During the second week, the staff could begin to teach the children mastered programs and easy programs. This relationship-building program did not solve every problem, but it sure helped.

SUMMARY

This section focused on the importance of human relationships and their role in teaching verbal behavior to children with autism. There are four key points to remember from this section.

1. Building relationships is important for the development of verbal behavior, because attention from others reinforces tacts, echoics, and intraverbals. If interactions between adults and children with autism are not reinforcing, your child cannot learn tacts, echoics, and intraverbals.
2. People become generalized conditioned reinforcers by being repeatedly paired with many different primary and secondary positive and negative reinforcers.
3. When building relationships with children who have autism:
   • Repeatedly pair yourself with many different kinds of reinforcers.
   • Pair various aspects of your behavior with many different kinds of reinforcers.
   • Be responsive to all of your child's approach behaviors.
   • Do not pair yourself with any aversive stimuli.
   • Get someone else to manage difficult situations.
4. Program generalization across different people. Make sure that your child has good relationships with everyone. If there are particular people that your child has difficulty relating to, implement a relationship-building program.

Ask Nicely!

OBJECTIVES

In this section, you will learn to:

1. Identify approach and avoidance mands;
2. Identify reinforcer assessment and reinforcer deprivation as key elements of mand training;
3. Describe the five common elements of mand training;
4. Apply reinforcer assessment and deprivation to mand training;
5. Describe how to prompt new mands;
6. Describe how to teach mands in the natural environment; and
7. Increase opportunities to mand by using incomplete and broken materials, controlling reinforcement, using incidental teaching, and teaching choosing as a mand.

The Mand

It is often easy to understand mands. Your child's behavior identifies the reinforcer that is powerful right now. What does it tell you if a child yells, "Bubbles!" looks at bubbles, and then reaches for bubbles? It is a good guess that bubbles are a reinforcer right here and now. You could use bubbles to teach a request to say, "More bubbles," "Bubbles, please," or "Blow bubbles." You would waste a great learning opportunity if you started teaching your child to ask for a book at that very moment.

Mand training is important for three reasons. First, children who do not communicate basic needs must have frustrating lives. They are at the mercy of other people guessing what they want. Every parent has experienced the exasperation of trying to figure out what a crying infant wants. Children who cannot request are in the same situation. Second, mand training pairs other people with known reinforcers. It may help to establish other people as generalized, conditioned reinforcers. Third, when children cannot mand with words or gestures, they may learn to mand in other ways, such as whining to obtain attention. They may learn to turn away and drop on the floor, instead of asking for a break. If you teach your child to mand in acceptable ways, he or she is less likely to learn to mand using problem behavior. If your child already has problem behavior, mand training may help decrease it.

You can mand for very simple things, like a snack, or for sophisticated secondary reinforcers, such as information. You can also ask for help or for someone to take something unpleasant away. Children who are just beginning a language program should learn to mand for the basics. Teach your child to mand for his or her top reinforcers. You can also teach children with better language skills to mand for more complex things, such as information, missing items, and help. In addition, you can teach them to mand in more sophisticated ways, such as using more grammatically advanced language. Table 1 summarizes a basic curriculum for mand training.

Approach and Avoidance Mands

There are two kinds of mands: approach mands and avoidance mands. *Approach mands* are reinforced by positive reinforcement. For example, when

TABLE 1
A Basic Curriculum for Mand Training

1. Mands wants by pulling, leading, and pointing.

2. Mands when someone else models the correct mand.

3. Mands for reinforcer when reinforcer is in sight.

4. Mands for reinforcer when reinforcer is not physically present.

5. Mands for others to perform an action.

6. Mands for attention.

7. Mands for missing item.

8. Mands using "Yes" and "No."

9. Mands using complete sentences.

10. Mands for help from others.

11. Mands for others to take an item away.

Note. From *The Assessment of Basic Language and Learning Skills* (ABLLS; pp. 23–28), by J. W. Partington and M. L. Sundberg, 1998, Pleasant Hill, CA: Behavior Analysts. Copyright 1998 by Behavior Analysts, Inc. Adapted with permission.

we point to an item, obtaining that item reinforces pointing. Or we say, "Hey!" and someone turns around. That reinforces saying, "Hey!" These are both approach mands. *Avoidance mands* are reinforced by removal of aversive stimuli. "No!" and "Maybe later" are both mands reinforced by removal of aversive stimuli. Children with autism must learn to use both approach mands and avoidance mands.

Analysis of the Mand

Mands are influenced by consequences, reinforcer deprivation, reinforcer satiation, and prompts for manding. Let us look at each of these in turn.

Consequences. You might think that everyone would reinforce a mand every time. However, we get busy, talk to other adults, and get involved in paperwork. So when a child mands, we may be too busy to reinforce that request. After a child with autism makes a request, an adult may sometimes say, "Wait," or say nothing at all. In this situation, the adult has missed an opportunity to teach the child to mand. Eventually, we all have to learn when it is the right time to ask for something and when to wait. Early on in teaching, you have to respond to every request promptly. Only later can you teach waiting and learning to request at the right time. When working with family members and staff on mand training with children, you should remove all distractions for the adults: Turn off cell phones, computers, and the TV. The next example shows why it is important to respond to a child's mands for current reinforcers

From Real Life
Reinforce That Mand!

The staff had put 5-year-old Erin's lunch in front of her several minutes ago. Usually she ate lunch quickly. This time, if you looked closely, you could see that something was wrong. Erin pushed her plate away little by little. If the staff asked her to eat, she would scrunch up her nose and turn away. Finally, the teacher breezed over and told Erin, "It's time to eat!" There was a long pause. "I don't want my goddamn lunch!" said Erin clearly. The teacher was surprised to hear this. But it *was* a clear mand! It took the teacher a couple of seconds to gather her thoughts. "OK, let's put it in the trash," said the teacher. Erin eagerly did so. The teacher made a mental note to teach Erin a nicer way to say no the next time she did not like her lunch.

Reinforcer Deprivation. The amount of time an individual has gone without access to the reinforcer maintaining a mand is a powerful influence on the frequency of the mand. Reinforcer deprivation has two effects. First, people work harder for the reinforcer. Second, it increases other behavior related to that reinforcer. Suppose you have not talked to anyone for a long time. Suppose also that talking to others is a reinforcer. Two things are going to happen. First, you will work harder for attention. If you call people on the phone and no one answers, you will probably keep calling until you talk to someone. Second, other behavior that was reinforced by attention in the past will increase. You will look out of the window to see other people. You will go through your phonebook. You may start hitting the speed-dial buttons on your phone.

Reinforcer Satiation. Think of this as just the opposite of reinforcer deprivation. Reinforcer satiation refers to a recent period of time when an individual has received a lot of the reinforcer that maintains the mand. Like deprivation, satiation has two effects. First, people will no longer work for the reinforcer. The thing that was once a reinforcer may even become a punisher. For example, you might turn away from your fourth helping of even a really good dessert. Second, satiation decreases behaviors related to the stimulus that previously was a reinforcer. For example, you might not ask for more dessert. You might not even look at the dessert tray.

The effects of reinforcer deprivation and satiation apply to all operant behavior, including mands. Thus, we may see mands for food right before lunch. We will also observe other food-related behavior, such as looking at food and food containers. After lunch, we observe fewer mands for food (e.g., people will not look at food or food containers).

The same rules apply to escape mands. If an aversive stimulus is intense and prolonged, then you will see more and more escape mands. You will also see other escape-related behavior, such as looking for places to escape the aversive stimulus. For example, suppose your child with autism finds new, crowded, noisy places unpleasant. If your child has to stay there for a long time, then you will see both appropriate and perhaps inappropriate escape mands. Your child will look for ways out of the unpleasant situation. Once the aversive stimulus is absent or reduced, you probably will not see these things. For example, if you take your child out of the noisy, crowded place for a short break every 10 minutes, then you will see much less of this behavior.

Prompts for Manding. We are more likely to emit mands when the reinforcer is nearby. When someone walks past with snacks, we are likely to ask for them. When we sit down and see a magazine across the table, we ask someone to pass it to us. Sometimes, we ask for things that are not physically present. Perhaps the mere presence of another person and reinforcer deprivation might be enough to cause us to request. If we are very busy and our printer runs out of paper, we might ask another person to get us some paper. We are unlikely to do this if there is paper in the printer, if there is no one else in the room, or if we are not trying to print something.

So, when you teach mands to your child, you should teach him or her *when* to ask for things. Part of mand training is to teach to mand in the presence of the right stimuli. Eventually, once children have learned that, they must also ask for things without the reinforcer being physically present. This is another example of generalization that we must plan for.

What This Means for Mand Training

Table 2 describes and gives examples of the five common elements in mand training. You must consider two things when teaching mands. First, use powerful reinforcers. You can use stimulus preference assessments to identify these powerful reinforcers. Second, use reinforcer deprivation. If your child likes food, then teach requesting food before and at lunchtime, not after lunch. Control access to favorite snacks and food. Do not give your child a bag of cookies during a class break. Give him or her a small piece of apple instead. Save the cookies for mand training later.

What should you do if your child does not look interested in the reinforcer? Do not train your child to mand for an item he or she is not interested in. There is no point to teaching that! Your child should learn to request a reinforcer only when he or she is reinforcer deprived.

The same rules apply to teaching escape mands. Suppose you want to teach your child to escape from long periods of difficult tasks. The first thing you must do is present difficult tasks without a break. You should only teach escape mands when your child is very motivated to escape. What should you do if your child is working hard and does not attempt to escape teaching? Do not teach your child to mand for escape in this situation. Your child will only learn to escape an aversive stimulus when the stimulus is present. The following From Real Life example illustrates this in a fun way.

From Real Life
Tickles!

Sergio wriggled, struggled, and screamed loudly. His ABA therapist would not stop tickling him. He had worked with Sergio for a long time, but had not taught him any escape mands yet. One day, he grabbed Sergio and tickled him as much as he could. He told Sergio, "Say, 'Stop,'" and continued to tickle him hard. The moment Sergio

TABLE 2
Examples of Five Tactics Used in Mand Training

Use effective reinforcers or aversive stimuli.	Use reinforcer deprivation.	Observe your child for an approach or avoidance response.	Wait for and/ or prompt the appropriate form of the mand.	Reinforce the appropriate mand form with the reinforcer your child requests.
Mary's dad knew that she loved for him to swing her around.	Dad did not swing Mary around all morning until going to the backyard.	Mary looked up at Dad and started to whine and stamp her feet.	Dad physically prompted Mary to stretch both arms up.	Once Mary had both arms up, Dad immediately picked her up, said, "Nice asking for up," and swung her around three times.
At 8:15 a.m., Ted, the new teacher, conducted a preference assessment using toys. He identified Julie's three preferred toys.	Ted put the three toys away in the closet. He waited until the last play session after lunch. During the last play period, Ted put the toys out in the play area on a shelf just a little too high for Julie to reach.	Ted saw Julie look up at one of the toys: a top. Then she reached for the toy.	Ted said, "Julie." She looked at him. Then Ted said, "Top."	Julie said, "t." Ted immediately gave Julie the toy, while smiling and said, "Nice asking."
Ben noted that his brother loved watching cartoons on TV.	Ben put on his brother's favorite cartoon. After 2 minutes, he stood right in front of the TV and did not move.	Ben's brother walked up to him and started to push him.	Ben asked, "What do you want?"	His brother finally said, "Move!" Ben immediately stepped out of the way.

(continues)

TABLE 2 (continued)

Use effective reinforcers or aversive stimuli.	Use reinforcer deprivation.	Observe your child for an approach or avoidance response.	Wait for and/or prompt the appropriate form of the mand.	Reinforce the appropriate mand form with the reinforcer your child requests.
The teacher ensured that all her children had preferred food at lunch time. She observed them carefully. If any of them pushed a food item away or left a food item, she asked their parents not to send that food item.	The teacher ensured that all her students had snacks only at break time. She scheduled break for an hour and a half before lunch. She ensured that the snacks were small.	Mohammed said, "Lunch" and pointed to his lunch bucket.	His teacher pulled his lunch bucket away from him, but held it where he could see it. Then she said, "Say, 'Give me lunch.'"	Once Mohammed said, "Give me lunch," his teacher immediately gave him his lunch bucket.
Yoko's after-school ABA therapist had noted that Yoko really liked to work on dinosaur books. He designed worksheets for her with questions about dinosaur pictures.	Yoko's ABA therapist showed Yoko her dinosaur book and worksheets at the beginning of the lesson. He scheduled the dinosaur worksheet for the end of her session. When he gave her the worksheet, he gave her pencils with broken points.	He noted that Yoko began to sigh and go through all the pencils. He waited until she looked at him.	Then he asked, "Do you need something?"	"Pencils," said Yoko. "What about the pencils?" asked her therapist. Yoko said, "Broken." "Yup, that won't work," said the therapist. He waited. Finally, Yoko said, "I need a pencil." "All right," said the therapist and immediately gave her a sharp pencil.

Note. All examples contain the same five steps: using effective reinforcers, using reinforcer deprivation, observing your child for an approach or avoidance response, waiting for or prompting a desired mand, and reinforcing with the correct reinforcer.

said, "Stop," his ABA therapist immediately stopped tickling him and put him down. Sergio quickly learned to say, "Stop."

Now he had learned his first escape mand.

Mand training should also teach stimulus control of mands. At first, you should teach to request for the objects that are physically present. Later, you should program generalization. For example, you might gradually fade the distance between your child and the object by progressively covering up the object. You might move your child away from the reinforcer in small steps. For example, when your child has not had a drink, you might wait for him to request a drink in the kitchen doorway with no drink present. Over time, you might increase the distance so that your child learns to ask for things in many different places.

Prompting New Mands

You can physically prompt mands that are gestures by, for example, pointing, using sign language, or handing over a communication card. If you physically prompt a correct mand, immediately reinforce both prompted and independent responses. Once your child reliably responds with a physical prompt, gradually reduce the prompt. For example, suppose you start by prompting a pointing response using hand-over-hand-over-hand prompting. Gradually move your prompt to the wrist, then the forearm, then elbow, and then shoulder. If your child starts to make errors, go back to an earlier stage of prompting. Then, continue prompt fading. You can also try to gradually reduce the physical pressure used in a prompt. Always use the lightest possible physical prompt that is still effective. A second way to fade physical prompts is shadowing. Shadowing involves gradually removing your hand from your child's hand while still keeping it very close to that of your child. As long as your child responds correctly, slowly increase the distance between your hand and your child's hand. If your child makes errors, go back to more intrusive prompting.

If your child reliably imitates words, you can use echoic prompts to teach mands. If your child approaches an object, you can prompt by telling him or her what to say. For example, if your child approaches a favorite book you should pull it away and say, "Book." When your child says, "Book," or an acceptable approximation, give your child the book within the next 2 seconds. Fade echoic prompts by gradually saying less of the word. Systematically drop the last sounds of the echoic prompt. For example, suppose your child now says, "Book" every time you prompt him or her to ask for a favorite book. Your fading procedure would involve gradually reducing your echoic prompt. You do this by going from "Book" to "boo," to "b." Only reduce the fading steps once your child has made a correct response several times with the current prompt. If your child makes errors, go back to an earlier prompt.

Here are some words of warning about prompting mands. Remember, you must only teach approach mands when your child is reinforcer deprived. If you prompt mands when your child is not reinforcer deprived, your teaching is likely to fail. So, ensure that your child is very motivated to request the thing that you are prompting him or her to ask for. If your child cannot imitate, echoic prompts will not work. In this situation you should probably use physical prompting of motor responses.

Extinguishing Old Mands

Sometimes we must get rid of immature forms of requesting. We do this to ensure that your child will mand appropriately. For example, suppose your child can effectively mand by leading you by the hand to get a favorite toy. If you now want to teach your child to point for the toy, your child will learn faster if you weaken leading *and* strengthen pointing. Do two things to reduce undesired mands. First, make the desired mand as easy as possible. Reinforce the desired mand immediately with the appropriate reinforcer. Second, do not reinforce the undesired mand. If your child leads you to the preferred item, do not respond or give him or her the desired item. If your child does not point independently, then prompt the point. Only respond when he or she points. We call this latter procedure *extinction.*

Extinction is the process whereby a previously reinforced response no longer produces that consequence. People often make the common mistake of thinking that extinction is the same as ignoring. Take a look at the definition of extinction again. What if getting a blue shoe reinforced the behavior? In this case, extinction means not getting the blue shoe for that behavior. What if getting a video reinforced the behavior? Then extinction means not getting the video. If the behavior was reinforced by escape from teaching, then extinction means no longer being able to escape. The way you do extinction depends completely on the reinforcer maintaining the behavior you want to reduce.

During mand training, you must know what the reinforcer is for the undesirable form of manding. You must ensure that it is not delivered for the old response. Only deliver it for the new, acceptable mand. Technically, this is called *extinction and differential reinforcement of alternate behavior.* This is because you are combining extinguishing one mand with reinforcing an alternate mand.

Extinction has some drawbacks. Sometimes there is a temporary increase in the old behavior. This is called an *extinction burst.* For example, your child might try to lead you to something several times before pointing to it. If you make an error and reinforce the old response during the extinction burst, you will make learning more difficult. Extinction is sometimes accompanied by a temporary increase in emotional behavior and aggression. For example, if you no longer reinforce leading, your child might cry and whine for a while. If an extinction burst occurs, you must persist and keep teaching until such behaviors are reduced and go away.

Practitioners combine extinction with reinforcing other behavior because your child will learn faster and because the problems of extinction are less likely. So, ensure that you reinforce appropriate manding quickly and effectively. If your child has severe behavior problems, you should get some professional help if you are going to use extinction.

Teaching New Mands

Sometimes we want to teach a child a new mand. If you are lucky, your child may already sometimes mand using the new response. In this situation, the program only has to prompt and reinforce the new mand. You are not teaching a new response. You are just increasing the frequency and correct use of an existing mand.

Sometimes, your child may not make the new mand at all. Because the new mand is not in your child's repertoire, you have to teach the new response by prompting and fading. For example, if your child only mands by whining, your first step might be to teach pointing to a favorite toy. You can do this using physical prompting and fading. Next, you might teach your child to tap a person on the arm, look at the person, wait for the other person to ask, "Yes?" and then point to a favorite toy. This chain of responses is unlikely to occur without a prompt, even if your child sometimes does some of these steps. Therefore, you must use physical prompting and fading to teach each step.

Here is a second example of teaching new mands. It involves combining an existing response into larger responses. If a child can say "d" and "a," you might be able to teach a new response: "Da." Later, you can teach another new response: "Dada." You can do this using the echoic prompts described above.

Here is a third example. It involves teaching a more grammatically complex sentence using echoic prompts. If your child approaches an adult and says, "Bubbles," you might prompt a more complex request such as, "I want bubbles." You can do this using an echoic prompt. You then fade that prompt. You can use this method to increase the complexity of your child's speech in many ways. For example, you might teach your child to use adjectives by prompting, "Big bubbles." You might teach your child to request something from someone else by prompting him or her to say, "Mom, blow bubbles."

Chaining Mands

A good way to increase the number of mands your child uses is to build a chain of mands. To do this, you must first find a powerful reinforcer. Then, you can build a chain of mands around access to that powerful reinforcer. For example, suppose that a child works hard to go out on a swing. Think of all the things your child can ask for in order to get to the swing. Here are just seven. You can probably think of more. Your child can ask to (a) go out; (b) go get his or her shoes and coat; (c) have someone hand him or her the coat; (d) have someone put the coat on them; (e) have someone open the classroom door; (f) have someone open the door of the building; and (g) have someone move out of the way of the swing by saying, "Excuse me," when an adult is standing in front of the swing. This simple chaining procedure can be used to increase the number and variety of your child's mands. There are also some interesting and clever ways to develop chains of mands. For example, you might take a reinforcer, wrap it in something, put this inside an envelope, put the envelope in a box, and put the box in a closet. Now your child has to make many requests to finally get to the reinforcer. Additionally, this procedure allows for many opportunities to teach several forms of verbal behavior along the way.

How To Teach Mands

Use Discrete Trial Teaching

It is possible to teach manding during discrete trial teaching at a desk or special teaching area. Discrete trial teaching consists of repeated, structured opportunities to learn and can make learning easy by breaking it down into small, manageable steps. Discrete trial teaching also provides many opportunities to practice. Table 3 lists the 10 components of discrete trial teaching.

Discrete trial teaching is an effective teaching method. It has been used for many years. However, if you teach mands using discrete trial teaching, you should do a couple of things to make it more effective. First, use

TABLE 3
The 10 Steps of Task Analysis of Discrete Trial Teaching

Behavior	Definition
Eye contact	The instructor makes eye contact with the student for a minimum of 1 second contiguous to delivery of a verbal instruction.
Readiness response	The instructor gives no verbal instruction until the student's body is oriented toward the instructor and his or her hands and legs are not moving.
Delivers instruction once	The verbal instruction is presented only one time per trial. Any repetition of the verbal direction either in full or in part is an incorrect teaching procedure.
Verbal instructions	The verbal instruction is delivered with clear articulation, and matches verbatim the specific verbal instruction designated for that program. Each instruction will be a specific set of words defined in each program as the discriminative stimulus.
Correction procedure	A predetermined gestural, physical, or verbal prompt designated for each program is delivered within 3–5 seconds of the verbal direction after a failure of the student to respond. The predetermined prompt should be used contiguous to any incorrect response that is given.
Appropriate reinforcement	Only correct responses will be consequated with a tangible reinforcer contingently on a correct response. The tangible reinforcer will be presented simultaneously with verbal praise. No tangible reinforcement will be provided for incorrect responses, or while the student is engaged in inappropriate behavior, even following a correct response.
Specific praise	The delivery of a behavior-specific statement is provided concurrently with delivery of reinforcement. For example, the instruction, "Touch nose," followed by the student making eye contact with the instructor is followed by praise such as, "Good, touch nose."
Immediacy of reinforcement	The instructor states the behavior-specific praise within 1 second following a correct response and continues to present praise for the correct response until after delivery of the tangible reinforcer.
Data collection	A plus or a minus is recorded on a data sheet after each trial.

(continues)

TABLE 3 (continued)

ehavior	Definition
tertrial interval (ITI)	Following the end of a trial (usually represented by the presentation of reinforcer or correction procedure), the teacher pauses for a minimum of 1 second before delivery of the next verbal instruction, beginning the next trial. The duration of the ITI must vary from trial to trial.

ource: Modified from Sarakoff and Sturmey (2004), and Dib and Sturmey (2007).

reinforcer deprivation and powerful reinforcers to ensure that your child really wants to request the items used. You will know that you have done this when you see your child reaching and manding for the preferred items. Second, carefully and deliberately program generalization from discrete trial teaching to the natural environment. There is no guarantee that generalization of manding from discrete trial teaching is just going to happen. For example, if you teach your child to request pencils during discrete trials, then you should ensure that your child gets lots of practice to request pencils at other times. Readers are encouraged to review the book on discrete trial training in this *How To* series.

Discrete trial teaching is very effective. However, many people think that it is not the best way to teach mands. This is because it can be hard to ensure that reinforcer deprivation has occurred prior to discrete trial teaching. Also, discrete trial teaching may not allow for teaching mands in natural environments. The next subsection describes how to teach mands in natural settings.

Train in Natural Environments

Each time your child approaches or avoids an object, place, or person is an opportunity to teach a mand. Your child approaches and avoids things in natural environments every day. For instance, suppose Sarah runs to the corner of her playroom to get something. You can ask her to point to it before she plays with it. If Sarah wants to sit at a table to color, you can ask her to point to the chair. When Sarah reaches to get another color, you can ask her to name the color she wants. When she is done and wants to get up, you can ask her to point to where she wants to go. In this example, the adult observed naturally occurring examples of reinforcer deprivation. The adult noted each naturally occurring approach or avoidance response. Then, the adult prompted and shaped mands.

Contrive Opportunities to Mand

Mand training in the natural environment can be very effective. However, sometimes there may not be enough teaching opportunities in the natural environment. Teaching may be more effective if we create more opportunities to teach mands. How can you do this? You have to make them happen.

You can create opportunities to mand in many ways. Here are some examples:

- Put reinforcers where they are easily seen, but hard to get. Put reinforcers on shelves, just out of your child's reach and in clear plastic bags. When your child starts to approach these reinforcers, wait until a request is made. If the child does not request, prompt him or her to do so. For example, when it is snack time, put the cup, straw, and soda at the side of the room. Wait for your child to approach the soda. Deliver each item one at a time. Only pour a little soda. This way your child will ask for the cup, straw, and soda and say, "More," many times.
- Find a highly reinforcing activity that needs several materials. Give only some of the materials. Wait for your child to ask for the thing that is missing. For example, give your child only one piece of paper to draw on. Do not give any pencils, erasers, or pencil sharpeners. Wait for him or her to ask. Or give your child a broken pencil so that he or she will have to ask for a sharp pencil or a sharpener.
- Create a problem accessing a powerful reinforcer. Wait for your child to request it. For example, stand in front of your child's bike when he or she wants to ride on it. Wait for the child to say, "Bike." Then stand in front of the bike and wait to hear, "Excuse me." Or stand in front of the bathroom door when your child wants the bathroom, and wait for him or her to ask for it.
- Present a mild aversive stimulus. Wait for your child to ask you to remove it. For example, turn on the noisy food blender. Wait for your child to say, "Quiet."

There are many ways to contrive opportunities for your child to mand. The next From Real Life example illustrates several creative and fun ways to get children with autism to request the things they want.

From Real Life
There Is No Such Thing as a Free Lunch!

Mrs. Martinez had taught children with autism for several years. She was pleased to see their progress. All of her students requested food.

Some pointed. Some used single words or signs. Some used three- to four-word sentences. However, there were times when they did not ask for things, even though she knew they could.

Mrs. Martinez had observed another classroom using a procedure to increase mands at lunchtime. So she thought she would give it a try.

First, she scheduled snack time a little earlier than she used to. She also ensured that snacks were not used as reinforcer in between snack time and lunchtime, except for one student who did not have any other reinforcers. This ensured that her students were ready to eat at lunchtime.

Second, when lunch was brought in, she had Tania, one of her teacher assistants, sit with the lunch buckets. Tania waited silently. Once in a while, Tania made a noise with the lunch buckets or commented on the delicious food. Tania waited until a student made a mand. Only when children pointed or asked did they get their lunch bucket—and only after they made a better request than the first time.

But that was just the beginning. Mrs. Martinez's students had to ask someone to open their lunch buckets for them. Another classroom assistant sat back silently with the forks, spoons, and plates. Again, the children had to mand to access the items they needed for lunch. Each time they requested, they had to say a little more.

After a couple of weeks, Mrs. Martinez was delighted to see her students manding "Lunch," "Open," "Fork," "Plate," "Spoon," "More," "Dessert," "Soda," "Water," and more. Over time, Mrs. Martinez taught her students to use more complex sentences, such as, "Gimme lunch" and, "I want more soda."

Control Access to Reinforcers

If you give your child a large amount of a reinforcer every time he or she mands, you will have few opportunities to teach mands. Your child may also satiate to that reinforcer quickly. If you give your child a small amount of the reinforcer, you will be able to teach mands many times and your child will not satiate so quickly to that reinforcer. The next From Real Life example illustrates the power of controlling the quantity of a reinforcer during mand training.

From Real Life
"Goldfish, Please!"

I observed Maria, a staff member, teaching Ari, a young man with autism, to mand for Goldfish crackers at snack time. Ari raised his hand, waited, looked at the staff and said, "Goldfish, please." At first, each time Ari did so, he got 10 to 15 crackers. Ari was too busy eating to mand again. When Ari did request them, his response was slow and sluggish. Ari barely raised his hand without a physical prompt.

So, we changed the procedure. Each time Ari manded for Goldfish, the staff only gave him one cracker. The first time this happened, he seemed quite surprised. You could even observe a little extinction burst. Ari tried to grab more Goldfish. Ari even got out of his seat and tried to sit next to the staff member who handed out the Goldfish. She made sure that those behaviors were extinguished. Ari never got any Goldfish for grabbing. Ari soon got the idea. Within 3 minutes, Ari raised his hand quickly and eagerly, without a prompt. Ari clearly said, "Goldfish, please!" As a result, we had many more teaching opportunities. Within 10 minutes, Ari learned to raise his hand without a prompt, wait, and say, "I want more Goldfish, please!"

Use Incidental Teaching

Incidental teaching is an effective strategy to teach mands. First, identify your child's powerful reinforcer. Ensure that your child does not have access to that reinforcer for some time. Next, present the reinforcers where your child cannot easily get them. For example, put the reinforcer just out of your child's reach. Then wait. Once your child approaches these items, you can then prompt the mand you want to teach. You can use the same procedure to teach rejecting mands. Again, identify things your child dislikes. Systematically present them. Wait for your child to make his or her typical rejection mand. Then prompt a better rejection mand. Here are some examples. When your child has eaten plenty, offer a large extra portion. Wait for your child to show his or her usual reject mand, such as turning away. Then prompt a better mand (e.g., to say or sign "No more, thanks"). Here is another example. Sit your child next to someone he or she does not like. When the child starts to show his or her usual reject mand, prompt the child to say, "Go away," or, "Excuse me."

Teach Choosing and "Yes" and "No"

Another way to teach mands is to offer choices between preferred and non-preferred items. Begin by making the best choices easy and obvious. Later make the choices less obvious. Use the following five-step procedure.

1. Place two items in front of your child. One should be clearly preferred. One should be unappealing.
2. Ask, "What do you want?"
3. When your child mands for the preferred item, withdraw both items for 5 seconds.
4. Present the nonpreferred item, and ask, "Do you want this?" If necessary, prompt your child to say, "No" or to shake his or her head.
5. Present the preferred item, and ask, "Do you want this?" If necessary, prompt your child to say, "Yes" or to nod his or her head. As with other procedures, you have to plan generalization. Think about opportunities outside of teaching when you can offer your child choices so he or she can practice saying both "Yes" and "No."

Increasing Mands

The purpose of mand training is to teach your child to request often. Children should request many different things from many different people in many different places. So, it is important to monitor your child's progress in using mands. You can use a variety of simple monitoring methods (e.g., golf counters or data sheets and graphs). See Figure 5 for an example.

Whose behavior are we measuring when we monitor a child's mand use? To a great extent this is a measure of *your* skill, creativity, and motivation. You can create many opportunities for your child to mand. A skilled teacher can get a child with autism to mand about three times per minute during a structured teaching session. That's about 90 mands per hour! You may see fewer during less structured times. However, if you are creative, you can greatly increase mands during unstructured times, too.

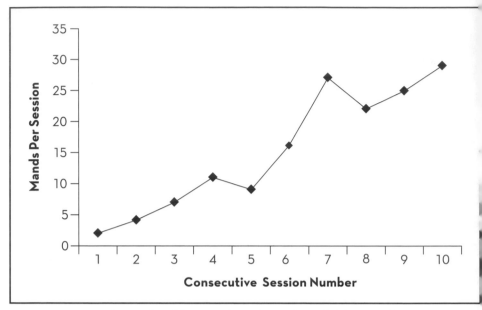

FIGURE 5. Sample graph of the number of mands a child emits during a training session.

SUMMARY

This section examined the teaching of mands. Here are the six highlights of this section.

1. Approach mands include pointing, leading, and requesting positive reinforcers. Rejecting mands include pushing items away, turning away, and saying, "No" in various ways.
2. To teach mands, you must identify positive reinforcers. Use preference assessments to do this. Then use reinforcer deprivation. This will increase the amount of mands and make reinforcing them more effective.
3. There are five common elements in all mand training:
   - Use effective reinforcers or aversive stimuli.
   - Ensure that reinforcer deprivation has occurred.
   - Observe your child's approach or rejection response.
   - Wait for and/or prompt the desired mand.
   - Reinforce the appropriate mand with the reinforcer your child requests.
4. Teach new mands using physical and echoic prompts. Fade these prompts as soon as possible. Ensure that errors do not occur during prompt fading.

5. Teach mands in the natural environment. Do this by carefully observing your child's approach and avoidance responses. You can improve mands by blocking and extinguishing less effective mands. You can also prompt improved mands.
6. Increase opportunities to mand with the following techniques:
   - Use frequent, small reinforcers.
   - Contrive opportunities for your child to mand.
   - Use incidental teaching.
   - Present incomplete and broken materials.
   - Present mild aversive stimuli.
   - Present choices between preferred and nonpreferred items.

Watching Other People

OBJECTIVES

In this section, you will learn to:

1. Define generalized imitation;
2. Recognize the importance of generalized imitation;
3. Teach generalized imitation;
4. Create a generalized imitation curriculum; and
5. Identify common problems in teaching generalized imitation and how to correct them.

What Is Generalized Imitation?

We often see people doing the same thing at the same time: The soccer crowd chants and roars at the same time. Everyone gets up when the minister enters. But they are not imitating. Why? Let us consider the definition of *generalized imitation*.

Four key features define *imitation*: (a) The model is presented before the learner imitates, thus the model evokes the imitative response. (b) The learner imitates the model within 3 to 5 seconds of the model. (c) The model and the learner's imitative behavior are the same or very similar. (d) The model must control the imitated response. That is, the learner copies whatever the model does.

Modeling can be planned or unplanned. In imitation programs for students with autism, we plan the modeling very carefully so that your child will imitate new things that other people do. Unplanned modeling occurs naturally without planning. For example, if all the children in a group clap at the end of a song, a child with autism may imitate clapping without prompts or programmed reinforcement. In this example, the clapping response occurs in the absence of a training program. So, it is an example of unplanned modeling.

A person is said to have a repertoire of generalized imitation when that person imitates novel responses that no one has ever reinforced before. For example, suppose someone sings a new song and your child imitates this new song without specific teaching to do so. Your child will have displayed an example of generalized imitation (Poulson, 2008.)

This definition of generalized imitation is very important. Unfortunately, most practitioners do not really understand it. It really is *unimportant* that a child with autism claps and puts a hand on his or her head when someone else does this. *What is important is that your child imitates new things without someone having to teach him or her to imitate each model.*

This emphasis on imitating new models without prompting or reinforcement has important implications for imitation programs. Imitation programs begin with an assessment of a child's current imitation skills. This must include models that no one has taught your child previously. Only when the trainer can show that your child imitates novel models can we say the imitation program really worked. Do not be impressed if your child imitates clapping hands, putting hands on head, touching knees, or a hundred other models. If your child cannot imitate novel models without prompting and reinforcement, he or she has not learned generalized imitation.

Why Is Generalized Imitation Important?

Generalized imitation is important for language development. Without imitating new things that other people do and say, a child is unlikely to learn much language. Researchers believe this is true for many aspects of language. Learning articulation, vocabulary, grammar, intonation, pitch, and voice volume may all depend on learning generalized imitation.

The same may be true of much social behavior. We often change our behavior according to what we see other people do around us. This is especially true in novel social situations. The first time we go to an event we have not experienced before, we anxiously observe what everyone else is doing. Even when we go to a novel social event within our own culture, we often look at what others do. If we are not sure how to use the metro card in a new subway system, we carefully look at what everyone else is doing with it.

One of the most important benefits of generalized imitation for children with autism is that it is extremely useful for teaching. We can teach almost any behavior with generalized imitation. We teach speech with echoic prompts. We teach vocabulary, grammar, reading, writing, social behavior, play, exchanging tokens, social behavior, and work skills with modeling. If your child has mastered generalized imitation, you can teach many different things quickly and easily.

There is a final reason to teach your child generalized imitation. Do you remember that the *echoic* is one of the basic verbal operants? Being able to model and match what someone says is a significant part of verbal behavior. Recall that there are two important differences between the mand and the echoic: First, the antecedent for the echoic is another person's vocal behavior. Second, the reinforcer is not something concrete (e.g., being given a token); rather, it is something abstract. The reinforcer for an echoic is the similarity between what you say and what someone else just said. Learning echoics is a big step in learning verbal behavior. It is also a big step in bringing your child in contact with other people. If children learn echoics, they learn that the things that other people say are important.

Teaching Generalized Imitation

In the 1960s, Professor Donald Baer and his colleagues (Garcia, Baer, & Firestone, 1971) developed the following general procedure to teach generalized imitation. It has been good ever since.

Identify Prerequisite Skills

The prerequisite skills for imitation training include (a) staying seated, (b) looking at the teacher, (c) keeping hands in lap, and (d) looking at objects. If your child does not reliably demonstrate these skills for at least three consecutive sessions, you should go back and teach these skills. Do not start imitation training until your child has mastered these skills.

Conduct Pretesting

Before imitation training begins, check to see if your child imitates three models that you might teach. Present all the models, and praise correct responses. Record correct imitations, approximations, errors, and no responses. Select those models that the child does not imitate reliably in three consecutive trials.

Use a General Trial Format

When we teach generalized imitation, we use discrete trial teaching. (See the previous section, Ask Nicely!, for a description of discrete trial teaching.) There are seven steps in teaching imitation with discrete trial teaching:

1. Ensure that your child sits, with hands in his or her lap, facing the trainer.
2. If you are doing object imitation, place one object in front of your child.

3. Say your child's name, pause, and say, "Do this."
4. Present the model.
5. If there is no correct response within 5 seconds or if the child makes an error, physically prompt the correct response.
6. Immediately praise prompted and unprompted correct responses.
7. Record the child's response after each trial. You should record if the response was independent and correct, a prompted correct response, an error, or no response.

During imitation training, select one of the models that your child did not master during pretesting. Select the model response that your child imitated the best. Use physical guidance and fading to teach these new models. See the previous section, Ask Nicely!, for descriptions of how to fade prompts. Continue training on this model until your child makes five correct unprompted responses. Then proceed to teach the next model. Once your child has mastered three models, conduct a postassessment. The postassessment should consist of 15 trials. Use five trials for each of the three trained models. If your child makes 14 of 15 correct responses, then your child has mastered these models. If your child imitates less than 14 of 15 models, go back and retrain.

Conduct Generalization Probes

Generalization probes are unreinforced trials. They are used to determine if your child has learned generalized imitation. Sometimes the trainer may mix probe trials with training trials. At other times the trainer may present probe trials in a block during postassessment. Mixing probe trials and training trials is preferable. This is because presenting blocks of unreinforced trials may result in extinction of imitation. For example, if you mix probe and training trials, your child will have plenty of chances to have correct responses reinforced on the training trials. This will be true even if your child always makes errors during every generalization probe trial. If your child has a block of 30 generalization probes and makes no correct responses, then the trainer will never reinforce your child's behavior. Your child might simply give up. Only when your child responds correctly and consistently to probe trials, has he or she learned generalized imitation.

A Curriculum To Teach Generalized Imitation

There are several kinds of models that your child must learn. These include (a) gross motor imitation, (b) fine motor imitation, (c) oral-motor imitation, (d) object imitation, and (e) vocal imitation. Teaching usually takes place in this order. Imitation training should include several examples of each type of model. For example, your child should learn several gross motor models, several fine motor models, and so on. Initially, select models that are very easy for your child to discriminate. For example, teach hands up versus hands down. Later, present models that are more difficult to discriminate, such as touch lips versus touch nose.

Program Generalization

Teaching generalized imitation is like teaching anything else. You must program generalization from the start. This means using varied trainers, locations, and materials. If you are teaching object imitation, you must use varied objects. If you have opportunities to teach imitation during naturally occurring activities, use them. If your child has mastered waving, make sure he or she gets to imitate waving "Bye" to everyone every day. If your child has some basic gross motor imitation skills, ensure that he or she models when singing "The Wheels on the Bus," and so on. Graph generalization data, as well as training data.

Learning generalized gross motor imitation does not lead to learning any other forms of imitation, such as fine motor or object imitation. Probe for generalization across different kinds of imitation. Do not be disappointed if your child does not imitate everything, even if he or she has mastered some forms of generalized imitation.

Common Problems and How To Fix Them

Imitation training is frequently done poorly. Practitioners often make two errors. The most important is that they incorrectly focus on imitation of specific reinforced responses. Second, they fail to realize that learning generalized imitation takes thousands of trials. It may easily take imitation training on 25 or more specific models to obtain generalized imitation. In Professor Baer's early research (Garcia et al., 1971), two children demonstrated generalized imitation only after learning 130 individual models. A third child learned much faster and acquired generalization after mastering only nine individual models. There are big differences among children in how quickly they will acquire generalized imitation.

Focus on Probe Trial Data, Not Training Trial Data

The only indication that your child has learned generalized imitation skills is when your child reliably imitates new models. Using probe trial data is the most important way to tell if your child is learning generalized imitation.

Irrelevant Stimuli

It is not uncommon to observe children making responses before the trainer presents the model. This is a big problem. These children are not imitating. Sometimes during teaching object imitation instruction, children make response when the trainer places the object in front of them. This is especially true if the trainer has taught only one action with that object. Children also sometimes respond to irrelevant cues. For example, a child may stand up as the teacher pushes her chair back, before ever modeling to stand up. When this happens, the child clearly has not learned to imitate. Even if the child only stands up after the teacher stands up first, it is still unclear which cue the child responded to—moving the chair or the model.

These problems are all the results of bad teaching. They are examples of failures to bring the child's imitation under the control of the teacher's prompts. To fix these problems, you must do the following three things. First, prevent pretrial responding. Only start the trial when your child sits with hands down. If your child begins to make any movement, physically prompt both hands back in his or her lap. Second, if your child is responding to irrelevant cues, go back and retrain. For example, suppose your child responds to the presentation of a block by banging it on the table and putting the spoon in a cup. You would have to teach imitating banging the block, banging the spoon, putting the block in the cup, and putting the spoon in the cup. This teaching procedure would remove irrelevant teaching cues. Third, if you must present irrelevant cues, ensure that they are not associated with imitating one particular response. For example, you may need a plane to teach imitating flying. You might need a toy car to teach imitating pushing. However, you should use other materials in subsequent training to teach these actions. For example, you could teach imitating many other actions with a toy truck and a doll. Similarly, you could teach imitating pointing, flying, and pushing with toy planes, cars, and dolls. If you do that, you will not present your child with cues other than the model you want your child to imitate. In that way, you will teach your child generalized imitation effectively. Some of these problems are quite hard to identify. It is good practice to get another person to observe your teaching. Another person can sometimes see inadvertent cueing that you may not know about.

Staff spend a lot of time on imitation training. If they focus on the graphs of teaching trials and do not include generalization probes, they often create a huge problem for themselves and the child. The next From Real Life example illustrates this problem.

From Real Life
One Hundred Percent on the Graph—Zero Correct in Real Life!

I was observing a staff member teaching imitation training in a preschool program. I had already reviewed the child's book of programs. It looked great. It seemed like this child had rapidly learned many imitation skills. As I observed the staff member teach the child, my heart sank. As the staff member moved his chair back, I could see the boy begin to get out of his chair before the staff member moved. After the little boy stood up, he began to sit down. The staff member put a block on the ground. The boy's hand began to point to the block before the staff member moved. I had bad news for the staff member: He was going to have to go back and teach all these imitation programs again.

I taught the boy myself. This time I removed the irrelevant cues. After we stood up, I modeled banging the block. He sat down. All he had learned was a response chain of stand up and then sit down. He had not leaned to imitate these models.

The graphs looked great, but the teacher had taught the child all the wrong things. He had not learned generalized imitation.

SUMMARY

This section considered the important topic of generalized imitation. Here are the six main points you should remember.

1. Generalized imitation refers to imitating *novel* models *without* reinforcement. Only when children do this have they learned generalized imitation.
2. Generalized imitation is an important foundation skill, related to learning language, social skills, and other essential skills. It is a very powerful teaching tool because you can show children what to do in many different circumstances.
3. Generalized imitation is important to verbal behavior because it makes sure that your child's behavior is influenced by other people's behavior. It establishes other people as relevant stimuli. You can also teach verbal behavior using echoic and other imitative prompts.
4. Instructors use discrete trial teaching to teach generalized imitation. Generalized imitation training uses massed practice on unmastered

models. The instructor takes probe data on novel models without re-inforcement to assess whether your child has learned generalized imitation.

5. The imitation curriculum includes gross motor, fine motor, oral-motor, object, and vocal imitation.

6. Common teaching problems include not focusing on probe data and providing too little teaching. Sometimes teachers establish the wrong kind of stimulus control. This occurs through inadvertent cueing. These problems can be fixed by using probe data, providing a large amount of teaching, and retraining models that have been incorrectly taught.

Say Something! Anything!

OBJECTIVES

In this chapter, you will learn to:

1. Understand why we teach vocalization;
2. Use Lovaas's four-step program to teach vocalization;
3. Teach entry behaviors for discrete trial teaching;
4. Differentially reinforce vocalization;
5. Reinforce higher rates of vocalization;
6. Increase the variety and complexity of vocalization;
7. Use variations on Lovaas's procedure to teach vocal mands; and
8. Describe alternatives to vocalization and the pros and cons of alternate methods of communication.

Why Teach Vocalization?

Communicating with speech has distinct advantages over other methods of communication. Almost everyone communicates through speech. It is the most conventional and widely understood way to communicate. If a person can talk, many people will understand him or her. There is another less obvious advantage to talking. It is very portable. There are no communication books to lose. There are no communication devices to carry around. There is no device to turn on and off.

Lovaas's Program To Teach Vocalization

Professor Ivar Lovaas (1981) developed a four-step intervention program to increase vocal behavior in children with autism. The four steps are as follows.

1. Reinforce any vocalization or looking at the adult with food. This should result in more vocalizations. It should also result in increased looking at adults.
2. Only reinforce vocalization if the vocalization follows the adult's vocalization within a few seconds. This should result in more vocalizations after the adult vocalizes.
3. Only reinforce vocalizations that occur after the adult vocalizes and the child's vocalizations approximates to what the adult says. For example, if the adult says, "Ma," the adult only reinforces the child's vocalization if it starts with "m." If the child says "d," the adult does not reinforce that response. If the adult says, "Da," then the adult only reinforces the child's vocalization if it begins with "d." If the child says, "m," the adult does not reinforce this. This process continues until the child imitates simple words and sound combinations. These usually include simple words such as "Mama," "Daddy," "Baby," and "Bubbles."
4. Once a few simple words are taught, new words are taught using echoic prompts and fading.

People have used this method for many years. Not all children with au tism learn to talk using this method. However, this is a good place to start

Entry Behaviors

Before you use this method, your child must be able to do certain things including (a) remain seated for an extended period of time; (b) keep his o her hands down; (c) look at an adult when his or her name is called; (d) imi tate an adult; and (e) show little problem behavior, such as aggression or ste reotypy. What should you do if your child does not have these prerequisit skills? You should teach your child these elementary behaviors using stan dard behavioral methods. These include simple manual prompting, fading prompts, and reinforcement. Establishing these entry behaviors will prob ably help if your child has behavior problems, because sitting quietly with quiet hands is incompatible with many behavior problems.

Differential Reinforcement of Vocalization

The second and third steps in Lovaas's (1981) program include differentia reinforcement of vocalization. What does this mean? First, your child mus make some sounds. These can be babbling or cooing. Often, early sound consist of those made at the front of the mouth, including vowels like "ah," "eeh," and "ooh." They also frequently consist of consonants made at the front of the mouth, including "m," "b," "d," and "p." Children may not say these sounds perfectly. That does not matter at first. You can shape these sounds later. To begin with, the most important thing is to get your child to make a lot of sounds often.

Differential reinforcement means only reinforcing some behavior and not reinforcing other behavior. In this case "differential reinforcement of vocalization" means reinforcing making sounds and not reinforcing silence. To make this procedure most effective, you should do the following: (a) Use effective reinforcers identified using a preference assessment; follow the procedures described in the section titled What Does Your Child Like? (b) Reinforce immediately. Deliver the reinforcer within 2 seconds of your child making each sound. (c) Reinforce every time. (d) Pair primary reinforcers with social interaction, such as smiling, praise, touch, or tickles. (e) Take data. Figure 6 shows you how to fill out a data sheet. Figure 7 shows you how to summarize the data. You can find a blank form in Appendix E.

Child's Name: _Dave_____ Date: _7/13/07_____ Time: _10:05 A.M._____

Reinforcer(s) Used: _Juice, tickles, praise_____

Time	Number of vocalizations
10:05	///
10:06	//
10:07	//
10:08	///
10:09	///
10:10	/////
10:11	///
10:12	//////
10:13	///
10:14	/////
Total	35

FIGURE 6. Completed vocalization recording form. *Note.* In this example, the number of vocalizations increases over time, suggesting that the procedure is effective.

Session	Number of vocalizations
1. 7/5/07, 3 P.M.	12
2. 7/5/07, 6 P.M.	15
3. 7/7/07, 10 A.M.	9
4. 7/8/07, 11:30 A.M.	9
5. 7/8/07, 2 P.M.	14
6. 7/8/07, 2:30 P.M.	17
7. 7/8/07, 4 P.M.	23
8. 7/11/07, 10 A.M.	25
9. 7/12/07, 4 P.M.	36
10. 7/13/07, 10 A.M.	35

FIGURE 7. Completed Data Summary Sheet for tracking vocalization instruction. *Note.* The number of vocalizations increases over time, indicating that the program is effective. Also note that sessions 3 and 4 were ineffective, as shown by the significant decrease in the number of vocalizations. This should alert you to change your teaching method in some way.

(f) Graph, analyze and use the data. If the data are going up—keep doing what you are doing. If the data are flat or going down—do something different. For example, change the reinforcer. (g) Start with short sessions. To begin with 5 minutes is fine. Gradually lengthen the session. Following this procedure should result in your child making lot of sounds. Once this happens, move on to Step 2 of Lovaas' procedure—only reinforcing making sounds after an adult make a sound.

Increasing Variety and Complexity of Vocalizations

What should you do once your child reliably makes a few sounds? Increase the complexity of what your child says. Do this in very small steps. If your child says, "b," "ah," and "ooh," you can begin to work on "Ba" and "Booh." To figure out what to teach, make a list of all the sounds your child makes.

TABLE 4
How To Combine Simple Sounds into More Complex Sounds

Child's current sounds	Possible sound combinations for instruction
b	baaah
p	ba
m	booo
aaah [long]	paaah
a [short]	pa
ooo [long]	pooo
	maaah
	ma
	mooo
	ooop

Note. Some of the sound combinations approximate actual words.

Then make a list of combinations of sounds that you could teach. See Table 4 for some examples.

There are several teaching methods you can use to teach more complex sounds. The easiest is to prompt and reinforce. If your child imitates and has learned to make sounds after an adult makes a sound, then you can use vocal prompts to teach more complex sounds. You should mix easy and difficult sounds. This will give your child continued experience of success and will keep your child interested in learning. Table 5 shows how easy and difficult sounds can be mixed within one teaching session.

Mand Training and Shaping Vocalization

Recently, two of my graduate students, Ben Thomas and Michael Lafasakis, developed the following procedures, which are extensions of procedures that Partington and Sundberg (2001) developed. Their procedure combines elements of Lovaas's (1981) ideas with teaching manding. They used this procedure with children as young as 3 years old who had autism. At the beginning of the studies, none of the children requested using words. Many of them only requested using reaching, grabbing, crying, and other undesirable forms of asking. After using this procedure, many could ask for

TABLE 5
How To Mix Easy and Difficult Trials

Trial	Target	Child response
1	b	+
2	aaah	+
3	b	+
4	aaah	+
5	baaah	−
6	baaah	+
7	m	+
8	ooo	+
9	m	+
10	ooo	+
11	mooo	+
12	mooo	+
13	b	+
14	baaah	+
15	m	+
16	mooo	+
17	baaah	+
18	mooo	−
19	baaah	+
20	mooo	+

Note. In this example, "b," "aaah," "m," and "ooo" are easy sounds. In Trials 1 through 4, the therapist begins with these mastered sounds. In Trials 5 and 6, the therapist combines the sounds. In trials 7 through 10, the therapist again uses mastered sounds. In Trials 11 and 12, the therapist combines these sounds. Look carefully at the remaining trials to see how the therapist systematically varies easy and difficult trials so that, in the end, the child imitates several new complex sounds reliably.

things they liked, using approximations to correct sounds, and sometimes with complete words.

To begin with, the therapist conducted preference assessments. This allowed them to find items the children would work hard for. The therapist also made an inventory of all the sounds the child made and then matched these sounds up with the preferred items. For example, if the child approached a book often in the preference assessment and sometimes said "b" or "d," those sounds were targeted as approximations for the child to learn. There are four phases in the procedure.

- *Phase 1: Nonverbal replacement mand training.* Here, the therapist prompts and reinforces new mands (e.g., pointing) and extinguishes current mands (e.g., throwing tantrums and whining). The therapist gives the child 3 to 5 seconds to make an independent response. Then, the therapist uses full physical prompts to get the child to point to the item with a finger. The therapist gradually fades these prompts from hand to elbow to shoulder. The therapist also models the sound as the child points. For example, suppose a child usually grabs his book. In this phase, he would not be allowed to get his book by grabbing. Instead, he would have to point independently or with a prompt to get it while the therapist said, "Book."
- *Phase 2: Looking.* After the child points to the item, the therapist moves the item close to the child's face. The child has to look at the therapist's face. When the child looks at the therapist, the therapist models the sound. Over time, the distance between the object and the therapist's face is gradually increased in four steps. In the last step, the therapist just moves the item after the child points. The child has to look at the therapist before obtaining the item.
- *Phase 3: Oral motor, lip, and sound approximation.* In this phase, the child must point to the object, look at the therapist for at least 1 second, and make an approximation to the movement and/or sound. The therapist reinforces successive approximations to imitating the model. If the child does not make a sound, the therapist repeats the prompt. If the child still does not repeat the sound, the trial ends without reinforcement. The therapist then starts a new trial.
- *Phase 4: Vocalizing the actual target sound.* In this phase, the child must point, look at the adult, and vocalize for the item. The therapist reinforces both prompted and independent vocalizations.

This program has been quite successful in teaching young children with no speech or minimal speech to request preferred items using words. It also appears to be an effective way of replacing unacceptable mands with acceptable vocal mands. It is distinct from Lovaas's (1981) procedure since it teaches mands, rather than echoics. One of the advantages of this is that mands may be more useful, at least at first. Vocal mands may also compete with unacceptable mands, such as tantrums. We are currently researching this method. There is no published research on this procedure yet, but i looks promising.

Alternatives to Vocal Communication

What can you do if your child cannot vocalize and does not learn throug] these standard methods? You can teach your child say something in som other way. There are several alternatives to talking. These include (a) sign language; (b) communication books; (c) visual communication systems such as PECS (2008); (d) electronic communication devices, such as com munication boards; and (e) writing. These alternatives differ in a numbe of ways. People understand some methods better than others. For example many people understand an electronic recording of a voice. Few people un derstand manual signing. Likewise, some forms of communication are eas ier for your child to access. For example, holding up single a card is faste than searching through a communication book with hundreds of pictures Some communication devices are clumsy and slow. If these communication devices are stored in backpacks or attached to wheelchairs—or worse yet stuffed in closets—communication can be slow. Teaching children with au tism to use these alternatives to speech requires a great deal of effort. You should select alternative communication devices cautiously. A great deal o time is sometimes invested in teaching a communication method that i understood by few people or that is difficult to use.

Alternatives as Temporary Measures

For some children, insisting that they speak may slow learning to commu nicate. Teaching pointing, some common signs, or some communication cards might be a very good way to start. For example, teaching mands using these methods might help eliminate undesirable behavior, give the child the general skill of requesting, or get your child interested in other people quickly. Therapists and parents can then use this as a basis to teach talking later on.

The important thing you must remember is that the alternative form of communication is a temporary measure. So, keep it temporary! If the long-term goal is to teach the child conventional speech, then the treatmen team must focus on *this* goal. It is easy to get distracted with your child's good progress on PECS or signing. You can put long-term goals for talking on the child's Individualized Education Program (IEP).

Alternatives as Permanent Measures

For some children, learning to talk is extremely difficult. A significant number of children do not learn to speak. Even good ABA does not teach all children with autism to talk. For some children, the long-term plan should be to continue to use an alternative form of communication. If that is the case, a lot of effort must go into training everyone around your child to learn the way the child communicates. For example, all classroom staff, peers, family members, and anyone else who works with the child must be fluent in understanding and using the child's method of communication. Also, practitioners must work hard to make the method of communication as easy as possible to use. For example, organizing the pages of a communication book or the layout of a communication board may make the device much easier and faster to use.

Listener Support

Recall that communication involves both speaker and listener functions. Most ABA programs focus on the *speaker's* behavior. However, the role of the *listener* is also crucial in any communication exchange. The listener does two important things. First, they reinforce the speaker's behavior. Second, they cue, or present antecedents, for the speaker to respond to. Let's look at each of these in a little more detail using the example that follows.

From Real Life
Good Speaker–Bad Listener

Lorrette says, "Video." Her dad is busy on the phone and says nothing to her. She says, "Video, please!" in a louder voice. Her dad looks around. She starts to cry. Dad puts down the phone and walks over. He asks, "What do you want?"

Lorrette is a great speaker. Dad is a lousy listener. Without thinking about it, he has extinguished appropriate requesting. Instead he taught his daughter to cry to get a video. If someone had trained him better and if he had given priority to Lorrette, his daughter would learn verbal behavior better.

That "real-life" anecdote is a simple example, but there are many subtleties. A responsive listener will look very carefully at the speaker's behavior for indications of things that are reinforcers. Of course, one should look for conventional mands to indicate which reinforcers to deliver. But one should also watch carefully for other things the child might find reinforcing. The listener should observe a child carefully for the things the child talks about most often and the things the child is most enthusiastic about. The listener should also carefully observe the things the child looks at, reaches for, says "No" to, and turns away from. The smart listener will use the information from these observations to support the speaker's behavior.

Presenting cues (discriminative stimuli) is the second listener function. A listener must present relevant antecedent stimuli that make the listener's appropriate verbal behavior more likely. Listeners must also remove antecedent stimuli that inhibit verbal behavior or that cue competing behavior. For example, a skilled listener will present verbal cues, such as references or questions about reinforcing topics. A skilled listener may also present physical cues to make certain kinds of conversation more likely. Think about how we use photos of babies, weddings, and vacations to prompt our own verbal behavior.

Certain cues promote inappropriate verbal behavior. A skilled listener avoids mentioning obsessional topics or physical cues for obsessional speech in order to make appropriate verbal behavior more likely. Some interventions carefully select physical stimuli, such as magazines and photographs and drawings of preferred items, in order to promote appropriate verbal behavior. Often they are placed physically close to the person. Sometimes they are built into work materials, such as photographic schedules.

Skilled listeners also present effective consequences for the speaker's verbal behavior, reinforcing the listeners' appropriate verbal behavior. They redirect inappropriate conversation or other behavior back to appropriate speech. An effective listener will (a) immediately reinforce appropriate speaker behavior, (b) extinguish inappropriate speaker behavior, (c) present cues (discriminative stimuli) to prompt appropriate speaker behavior, and (d) remove cues (discriminative stimuli) for inappropriate speaker behavior.

SUMMARY

This section described ways to teach basic and more elaborate speech to children with autism. There are seven important points to remember.

1. You should teach vocalization because it is the most conventional form of communication, understood by most people, and may decrease problem behaviors.

2. Lovaas's four-step program to teach vocalization includes reinforcing any vocal behavior. The therapist then brings vocal behavior under the stimulus control of other people. This is done by only reinforcing vocal behavior after another person speaks. Later, the therapist differentially reinforces child vocal behavior after the adult speaks. Finally, the therapist shapes accurate child imitations of more complex forms of vocal behavior.

3. Before teaching verbal behavior, it is important that you teach your child to sit and look when his or her name is called. You can elicit these responses with prompting, reinforcement, and shaping.

4. You differentially reinforce vocalization by doing two things. First, you only reinforce vocalization. Second, you withhold reinforcement for not speaking.

5. You reinforce higher rates of vocalization by doing two things. First, you reinforce higher rates of vocalization. Second, you withhold reinforcement for lower rates of reinforcement. Over time, you gradually increase the required rate of vocalization.

6. You can increase the variety and complexity of vocalization by combining existing sounds. If your child imitates, then you can use echoic prompts and fading echoic to teach new sounds and words.

7. There are several alternatives to vocalization. These include signing, various visual systems, and electronic communication devices. They all vary in terms of how easily other people understand them and how easy they are for your child to use. You have to make a balanced decision for your child as to whether or not to use them and what the purpose of using them is.

What's That?

OBJECTIVES

In this section, you will learn to:

1. Describe receptive language in terms of discrimination;
2. Describe matching, simple discriminations, and conditional discriminations and their relationship to receptive language;
3. Define the tact and its controlling variables;
4. Describe tact training using both echoic prompts with fading and mand training with fading; and
5. Describe feature, function, and class training as examples of conditional discrimination training.

Receptive Language

How do we know that someone really understands something? If you say something to me in English, I can repeat it, answer questions about it, and summarize it in spoken and written words at the right time. Suppose a child says, "Goggie," near actual dogs, pictures of dogs, and dogs on the TV and only says, "Goggie," to these stimuli and not to horses, birds, and apples. Most people would say that this child understands what a dog is. Professor Claire Poulson wrote, "*Meaning* refers to use in context" (Poulson, 2008). Receptive language reflects what we observe people do, not what is in their heads. Suppose I ask my students, "What is a reinforcer?" If they say, "You present the reinforcer and then the child makes a correct response," I would say they do not understand the idea of a reinforcer. This is because they made the wrong response for the context of that question. If I had asked them, "What is a discriminative stimulus?" I might say they understood the idea.

Matching and Language

Discrimination is the simplest form of receptive language. Suppose a child reliably points to a circle when I say, "Circle," and to a square when I say, "Square." You would probably say that the child understands *square* and *circle*. But if the child also points to an oval when I say, "Square," or does not respond correctly when I say, "Point to the round one," then we would say the child does not quite understand *circle* yet. This example shows that simple discrimination is the beginning of receptive language.

Simple Discrimination Training

A simple discrimination refers to a situation in which the same response is always made to a stimulus. An example is always pointing to the dark figure on a white piece of paper. This is a simple discrimination because the same response is made each time. In simple discrimination, the therapist reinforces pointing to the figure every time. If the child points to the white background, the therapist does not deliver reinforcement. This is often a good place to start discrimination training.

Conditional Discrimination Training

A more complex kind of discrimination is conditional discrimination, in which the therapist presents one of several discriminative stimuli. The therapist might present spoken words, such as "Cat," "Dog," and "Cow," or set of *comparison stimuli*, such as pictures of a cat, a dog, and a cow. Now, when the therapist says, "Cat," the therapist only reinforces pointing to the picture of the cat. If the child points to the dog or the cow, the therapist does not reinforce these responses. When the therapist says, "Dog," he or she reinforces only pointing to the picture of the dog. The therapist no longer reinforces responses that had been reinforced during previous trials. Thus, the term *conditional* describes the nature of the relationship between the presentation of the sample stimulus and which response is reinforced. The response that the therapist reinforces is conditional or depends on the discriminative stimulus that the therapist presents.

Notice here how children who make conditional discriminations begin to look like they have receptive language. You would say that children understand *dog, cat,* and *cow* if they accurately point to pictures after someone says these words. To some extent, teaching receptive language is just an elaboration of these conditional discriminations. You can increase the number of classes of stimuli trained. For example, you might add in classes of stimuli, such as the sounds that the animals make, photos, video clips, cartoons, words written in lowercase and words written in uppercase. You might also add in other verbal stimuli, such as "Feline," "Canine," and "Bovine," or, "Who says, 'meow'/'yap'/'moo'?" If you saw a child make many accurate conditional discriminations among these classes of stimuli, you might say that he or she *really* understands ideas like *dog* and *cat* and *cow*.

Generalization

Programming generalization for receptive language from the beginning is essential. Your child has to learn to label thousands of new pictures, photographs, line drawings, movies, video clips, and actual objects that he or she has not learned to label during teaching. When setting up any program to teach receptive language, think about generalization from the beginning. What do you want to teach the child to label: photos, line drawings, actual objects, or all of them? Then design a large bank of stimuli. Use some for teaching and the rest for generalization probes. Remember, only when your child starts to label the generalization stimuli without training is your child really beginning to make important progress.

The Tact

In everyday language, a tact is a label. A tact labels a sensory experience. Skinner (1957) used the word *tact* because it described how this verbal operant makes con*tact* with the environment. We should be able to label the sight of a car. We should also be able to label the smell, feel, and sounds associated with a car.

A more technical definition of the tact is that it is a verbal operant. It is a behavior reinforced by its consequence. It is reinforced by interaction from other people. The tact's antecedent is nonverbal. That is, the discriminative stimulus for the tact is the object that is labeled. Table 6 illustrates this point. There are many forms of tacts. They include nouns ("It's a *car*"),

TABLE 6
The Antecedent, Behavior, Consequence (ABC) Model for Tacts

Antecedent	Behavior	Consequence
A car	"That's a car!"	"Yup, it's a car."

verbs ("It's *moving*"), physical relationships between objects ("It's *behind* the truck"), properties of objects ("It's *red*"), and actions ("It's moving *slowly*"). You can see from all these different kinds of tacts that there is a lot to learn. Consider the sentence, "The big red car is behind the truck, moving slowly." How many tacts are there in that one sentence?

Some tacts refer to things that are invisible. When we say, "I am hungry," "My head hurts," or "I am tired," we tact stimuli inside our skin. Only one person can observe these stimuli: the one who is hungry, whose head hurts, or who is tired.

See Table 7 for further examples of tacts. Even the few tacts shown can generate many sentences. Each sentence may contain a few or many tacts.

This definition of the tact has two important implications for teaching. The first is that the child must be able to make many discriminations to use tacts effectively. Just look at the second column in Table 7. To tact just the four words correctly in the second column, your child must discriminate *car* vs. *cat*, *car* vs. *house*, *car* vs. *tree*, etc. The second implication is that the reinforcer that maintains tacts is social interaction. If interaction is not a reinforcer for your child, then your child cannot learn to tact. Remember from the section titled Other People: You Gotta Love 'Em that establishing people as reinforcers is an essential part of learning verbal behavior.

Teaching tacting private events, such as hunger, is especially difficult because the person doing the teaching has to guess what is going on inside the child's skin. Many of the discriminations relating to tacting private events are also subtle. We all have difficulty accurately tacting *tired*, *anxious*, *worried*, and *depressed*.

TABLE 7
Example of How Numerous Sentences Can Be Generated from a Few Tacts

Adjective	Noun	Verb	Adverb
(The) big	car	moves	well
small	cat	hops	badly
yellow	house	eats	quickly
green	tree	runs	sadly

Note. Try to figure out how many conditional discriminations someone has to make to generate all the sentences hidden in this table.

Tact Training with Echoic Prompts

The easiest way to teach tacts is to use echoic prompting and fading. For this to work, your child must imitate spoken words. Here are four steps for you to follow.

1. Present the object near the child.
2. Prompt the correct tact with an echoic prompt, "Car."
3. Reinforce correct responses with praise.
4. Fade the echoic prompt gradually ("Car" → "Ca" → "C").

Fade prompts gradually. Your child should make several correct responses at the current level of prompting before you fade the prompt to the next step.

There are other important considerations. First, you might teach several tacts within a teaching session. If you do, at the beginning, make the objects and the words very different from each other. Teach "Car" and "Bubbles," not "Cookie" and "Carrot." Later, you can make the teaching more difficult. You can do this by making the objects and sounds similar. Second, you might have to use task interspersal with some children to keep their interest. For example, you might mix in some easy, mastered tasks with some tact training trials. Then, you may want to fade in other verbal prompts along with the object, such as, "What is this/that?" This may be done later after the tact is acquired.

Tact Training with Mands

A second way to teach tacts is to begin with existing mands using the following three-step procedure.

1. Present the motivating operation. Make sure your child is deprived of the relevant reinforcer. For example, do not give any bubbles for 5 minutes before teaching. Present an echoic prompt: "Say, 'Bubbles.'" When your child emits the correct response, reinforce it with the specified reinforcer. Blow the bubbles.
2. Fade the motivating operation. That is, gradually use less and less deprivation of bubbles. Present the echoic prompt: "Say, 'Bubbles.'" Reinforce the correct response with praise only.
3. Fade the echoic prompt. Just present the object. Praise correct labeling.

Tact training using existing mands can be complicated. It is essential that the teacher fade both reinforcer deprivation and echoic prompts. It is also essential that praise is a sufficiently powerful reinforcer to maintain tacts, after those responses had previously been maintained by other rein-forcers, such as food or preferred activities.

Teaching Feature, Function, and Class

We make many discriminations concerning stimuli around us. We discrim-inate the features, functions, and classes of stimuli. When we ask, "Which one has ink in it?" we present a discriminative stimulus for the response, "The pen." When we ask, "Which one do we write with?" we present another discriminative stimulus for "The pen." When we ask, "Which one belongs in school?" we present yet another discriminative stimulus for "The pen." The responses to these questions are also tacts. So, remember that these re-sponses are reinforced with praise and interaction.

Suppose now we have several items on a desk in front of a child. Let's say we have two drinks (grape soda and lemon juice) and two toys (a red car and a black video game). For each of these, we can identify discrimina-tive stimuli. These can be questions or descriptions of the object's features, what it does, or what class of things it belongs to. You might think of a wide range of verbal discriminative stimuli for these objects. Tables 8 and 9 give examples. You can do feature, function, and class teaching with objects, ac-tions, and pictures. This is nothing special; it is just another example of conditional discrimination training.

TABLE 8
Examples of Discriminative Stimuli for Feature, Function, and Class of the Items Grape Soda, Lemon Juice, a Red Car, and a Black Video Game

	Discriminative stimuli
Feature	Which is purple/yellow/red/black?
	Which is sweet/sour?
Function	Which do you drink?
	Which do you pour?
	Which do you drive?
	Which do you watch?
Class	Which is a drink?
	Which is a fruit?

TABLE 9

Examples of Discriminative Stimuli for the Form, Function, and Class of a Green Ball When Watching Another Person Bouncing a Ball

	Discriminative stimuli
Form	"Which one is round?"
Function	"You can bounce a . . . ."
Class	"Which one is a toy?"

SUMMARY

This section described receptive language as discrimination training. It also described how to teach receptive language using conditional discrimination training. Remember the following six points about receptive language.

1. Receptive language is a form of conditional discrimination. We say that someone really understands something if he or she makes many conditional discriminations in the right context.
2. Simple discriminations involve a response that is always correct. For example, pointing to a black square on a white page when someone says, "Point."
3. Conditional discriminations are more complex. Here, the correct response differs depending on the prompt (discriminative stimulus). When someone makes many accurate discriminations, we say he or she has good receptive language.
4. The tact is a verbal operant made in response to a nonverbal stimulus, such as the presence of an object. Social interaction is the reinforcer maintaining tacts.
5. Children learn tacts either by (a) presenting and fading echoic prompts or (b) using mand training and fading motivating operations and echoic prompts.
6. You can teach your child to tact the features, functions, and classes of objects using conditional discrimination training and reinforcing correct tacts with praise.

"The Wheels on the Bus Go . . ."

OBJECTIVES

In this section, you will learn to:

1. Define and give an example of the intraverbal and its controlling variables;
2. Teach intraverbals; and
3. Describe the limitations of teaching intraverbals to children with autism.

The Intraverbal

So far, the verbal operants we have considered have a simple relationship to their controlling variables. The mand is reinforced by the reinforcer it specifies. The echoic corresponds exactly to the model. The tact labels its stimulus. In these examples, stimulus control is relatively simple. However, verbal behavior is often more complicated.

> THEO: Mary is so . . . so . . .
> ANNE: . . . nosey!
> THEO: Yes! She asks all the wrong questions.

In this little example, each thing that is said is closely tied to what the previous person said, yet it has no physical resemblance to what is said. None of the words that follow has anything physically in common with the words the previous person said. Yet, they all make perfect sense. Suppose that after the first question, Anne had said, "There are 8 million people in the metro area." That answer would be weird. If she had said that, Theo would probably have given her a strange look. He might have asked if she knew what she was talking about! If Theo had first said, "New York is huge," then what she said would have been just fine. This illustrates that a lot of verbal behavior is under the stimulus control of the behavior of the previous speaker. However, most of our verbal behavior does not correspond in any simple way to what was previously said.

Skinner (1957) defined the intraverbal as a verbal operant that does not have "point-to-point" correspondence with what was previously said. Social interaction reinforces the intraverbal. Note that unlike the tact, the objects or events described are not physically present. In the example above, nosey Mary is not present. It is not the presence of nosey Mary that is the discriminative stimulus for the next verbal response; it is the previous speaker's verbal behavior that is the discriminative stimulus.

Like several other verbal operants we have discussed, it is social interaction from others that reinforces the intraverbal. When Anne says, "So nosey!" that reinforces the other person's verbal behavior. It is Theo's immediate social interaction that reinforces Anne's verbal behavior.

There are many kinds of intraverbals. For example, filling in the gaps of sentences that are incomplete. For example, when a teacher says, "The wheels on the bus go. . ." and the child says, "Round and round," the child's response is an intraverbal. It is an intraverbal because it does not correspond exactly to "The wheels on the bus" and because interaction from the teacher reinforces this verbal behavior.

You can think of many word associations as intraverbals. For example, if a teacher says, "Farm," the child may say, "Pig . . . farmer . . . the farmer's wife."

Finally, answering some kinds of wh- questions are also interverbals. For example, answering "What do you eat?" or "When do you eat?" or "What else do you eat?" are also examples of antecedents for more complex child intraverbal behavior.

Teaching Intraverbals

You can teach intraverbals using a three-step procedure similar to that described in the previous section, What's That? Start with existing mand teaching. Then fade out reinforcer deprivation and the echoic prompt.

1. Present the motivating operation. Ensure there is no social interaction for 5 minutes before teaching. Then present the discriminative stimulus, "The wheels on the bus go . . . ," and then the echoic prompt ("Say, ''round and 'round'"). When the child emits the correct response, reinforce it with praise ("Yes! That's right!").
2. Fade the motivating operation. (That is, gradually move to no deprivation of bubbles). Present the echoic prompt ("Say, 'Bubbles'"). Reinforce the correct response with praise only.

3. Fade the echoic prompt. Just present the verbal antecedent ("The wheels on the bus go . . ."). Then praise a correct response.

A Word of Warning!

There is much less research on teaching intraverbals than there is on teaching other aspects of verbal behavior. We have much less science to guide our practice here than in other areas. Teaching intraverbals is also a much more complex verbal operant to teach. Partington and Sundberg (2001) warn against teaching intraverbals too soon. They recommend that only children with extensive repertoires of echoics, mands, and tacts begin learning intraverbals. So, focus on teaching an extensive repertoire of all these other functions first, before teaching intraverbals.

SUMMARY

In this short section, we learned four main things about the intraverbal. They were as follows.

1. The intraverbal is a verbal operant that does not have one-to-one correspondence with its preceding verbal antecedent. Social interaction reinforces intraverbals.
2. Examples of intraverbals include filling in the gaps in incomplete sentences and answering some wh- questions.
3. You can teach intraverbals by beginning with mand training and fading out the motivating operation and echoic prompt.
4. Children with extensive repertoires of echoics, mands, and tacts are good candidates for learning intraverbals.

Last Words on Verbal Behavior

OBJECTIVES

In this chapter, you will learn to:

1. Identify two more verbal operants: the textual and transcription;
2. Recognize variability in verbal behavior and interventions to increase variability;
3. Use other aspects of communication, such as gestures and affect;
4. Heed words of caution concerning moving too fast;
5. Consider the difference between form and function in verbal behavior;
6. Recognize the importance of well-trained staff; and
7. Use the Internet to get educated about verbal behavior.

Two More Verbal Operants

Skinner's (1957) odd definition of verbal behavior said that verbal behavior was reinforced indirectly by the behavior of other people. Skinner extended his definition of *verbal behavior* to include reading (the textual) and writing (transcription).

The Textual

When your child reads a written word aloud, you might smile approvingly or say, "Uh-huh." Praise and other kinds of interaction may reinforce reading aloud. So, it is verbal behavior. Skinner called this verbal operant the *textual*. The antecedent for the textual is the written word. The response corresponds to the written word exactly, except that the response is spoken, rather than visual. The reinforcer is interaction and praise from another person.

You can read aloud and understand little. If you can read this text aloud, you can probably read Romanian aloud fairly accurately. However, most of us would not understand too much of what we said! Remember from earlier in the book that understanding refers to responding in context. This refers to manding, tacting, and using intraverbals correctly. You can emit mands, tacts, and intraverbals related to the text you are reading now. So, we would say, "You understand the book." Suppose you had to mand, tact, and emit intraverbals to text in Romanian. Most of us would not do very well. We would say that we really do not understand Romanian. We might say we were just parroting the text. So, as with other verbal operants, you have to teach each one separately from the others.

Transcription

Correctly writing down what someone else has said is the last verbal operant we will discuss. Here, the discriminative stimulus is the other person's spoken word. The verbal operant is writing the word. Again, the reinforcer is praise or other social interaction. Note that, like the textual, the response corresponds closely to the antecedent, but is not exactly the same. The antecedent is spoken. The response is written.

Again, transcription does not imply understanding. You could probably write down some badly spelled words of Romanian. With practice, you could learn to spell them accurately, too. Like with the textual, you would not understand what you had written.

Intervention for Reading and Writing

ABA has had little to say about teaching reading and writing to children with autism. Behavior analysts designed the Edmark curriculum (EnableMart, 2008) many years ago. Some ABA researchers have developed clever ways to fade stimuli, such as line drawings into written words. However, the recent flourish of interest in verbal behavior has paid little attention to teaching textuals and transcription to children with autism.

Let's Talk About Something Else!

Variability is an important aspect of verbal behavior that should be given more attention. Some children with autism talk about a limited range of topics or repeatedly ask for the same thing. So, although they have spoken language, their verbal behavior is still odd. Fortunately, variability is just like any other aspect of behavior: It is influenced by its antecedents and consequences. You can measure and graph variability. For example, you can count the number of different things said or the number of responses that are different from the previous response.

The simplest way to increase variability is to reinforce novel responses. That is, each time your child says something new and different, reinforce it. One of my graduate students, Dr. Ron Lee, (Lee and Sturmey, 2006) did a series of studies using a variant of this procedure. He asked children with autism, "What do you like to do?" Many children always gave the same answer. He then reinforced a response only if it was different from the previous response. This simple procedure was often effective in teaching these children to say different things, though it assumes that the child can say other things. Sometimes it may be necessary to teach the child other words. If you do this, you can be sure that your child has other responses in his or her repertoire and that it is possible for him or her to say something else.

Another approach to variability is to prompt new responses. This can be done by presenting interesting things to talk about and prompting talking about these other things. Scripting and fading scripts can also be an effective way to get children with autism to say new things. You can find descriptions of scripting and script fading in Lynn McClannahan and Pat Krant's (2005) useful book, *Teaching Conversation to Children with Autism: Scripts and Script Fading.*

Other Aspects of Communication

Verbal behavior does not occur in isolation from other aspects of behavior. When we communicate we use gestures, facial expressions, and adopt conventional postures. We also show affective behavior, like smiling and frowning, which is in synch with what we say. Teaching children with autism to talk about things that are of interest to their communication partner is also important. Your child with autism must be reinforcing to others. Teaching children with autism to talk or otherwise communicate is not enough.

Without appropriate gestures, posture, and affect, your child might still appear unusual. You should teach your child these behaviors as well. Your child can learn them just like other responses. Modeling and reinforcement can be effective ways to teach these behaviors. Some of the behaviors can be tricky and subtle. Nevertheless, you can teach these aspects of communication.

You must make sure that your child with autism is interesting to others to approach and talk to. Make sure your child is attractive to others. Make sure that his or her clothes are clean, neat, and fashionable. Look at the clothes that other kids in mainstream classes wear. Make sure that your child's clothes do not label him or her as different or immature. Make sure your child is clean. Make sure that your child does not do anything that might offend others. If he or she does, ensure that your child learns to do something better. Teach your child to be nice to others. Your child could offer toys to peers and compliment staff. For example, I have had some success teaching teenagers with autism to begin talking about sports and popular TV shows. This can make what they say more interesting to their typical peers. Others have taught children with autism to reinforce their peers' behavior by offering gum, handheld games, and other reinforcers for their peers' approach behavior.

Do Not Go Too Fast

There is a lot to learn when teaching verbal behavior. Remember, it takes typically developing children years to learn to use verbal behavior effectively. In some ways, we are all still learning verbal behavior, even as adults. It is tempting to say that children with autism have made more progress than they really have made. I have seen many examples of this. Teaching verbal behavior to children with autism is an enormous and daunting task. Do not say that your child has learned anything more than he or she actually has. When you do that, you fool yourself. Worse yet, you cheat your child out of the education he or she needs.

Form Versus Function

"Let's go for coffee!" It sounds like a mand for coffee, right? Or is it an escape mand to end my tedious work? Or is it a mand for social interaction, so I can go talk to my colleagues for a while? The form of the verbal behavior does not tell you its true function. Maybe "Let's go for coffee!" is not a mand at all. Maybe it is a tact that labels the time of day. Do not be fooled by what you hear! We often assume that we can tell what kind of verbal operant someone has just emitted by its form. But we may be wrong. This is not a mere academic quibble. It is a very practical problem. For example, if you really want to teach tacts, then social interaction must be the reinforcer maintaining the verbal behavior. If you reinforce correct labeling with food, then you may be simply teaching an odd kind of mand that looks like a tact, but is a mand for food.

These problems affect your child's teaching. You might think you are teaching your child to tact. But maybe your child is just learning to mand.

These are sometimes difficult problems to unravel. Often an outside person with good training is the best person to help with this. I have fooled myself many times. Remember, verbal behavior is about function—Skinner's (1957) six verbal operants—not the form of what is said.

Get Well-Trained, Qualified Staff

ABA services have a big problem. Demand for services greatly outstrips the supply of well-qualified staff, and the number of children entering early intervention services and special education classes continues to increase. Parents whose children receive high-quality early intervention services expect high-quality special education services, too. Soon, parents whose children receive effective education will expect better services for their adult children with autism.

There are now many service providers, including services for profit. Some services are excellent. Others are motivated by profit and care little about the quality of the services provided. The quality control of ABA services is variable.

Teaching some aspects of verbal behavior is relatively easy; however, teaching other aspects of verbal behavior requires precise, complicated, and flexible skills. Whether the teaching involves simple or complex skills, staff delivering the teaching must be effectively trained. Unfortunately, too many staff, even those with professional qualification, are poorly trained. Parents cannot always tell the difference between good and bad services. To help ensure that a child receives good services, parents should make sure that their staff are well trained in ABA. Board Certified Behavior Analysts (BCBAs) may have better training than many practitioners do. If the staff who are working with your child are not BCBAs, try to get services in which the supervisors are BCBAs. If you cannot get BCBAs, look for practitioners who have had graduate classes in ABA, attend conferences on ABA, and are involved in state ABA organizations.

A list of helpful Web sites follows:

Local chapters of Families for Early Autism Treatment (FEAT) can be helpful to learn about ABA. You can find information on the Web at http://www.feat.org/.

Local ABA chapters are on the Web at http://www.abainternational .org/chapters.asp.

Your school district might provide you with training and consultation if it is on your child's Individualized Education Program (IEP). A great resource for parental rights under the Individuals with Disabilities Education Improvement Act (IDEIA, 2004) and

what should be on your child's IEP can be found at http://www
.wrightslaw.com/.

You can find a list of local BCBAs at www.bacb.com/becom_frame
.html.

SUMMARY

This section described some of the outstanding issues related to verbal behavior.

1. There are six verbal operants: the echoic, mand, tact, intraverbal, textual, and transcription. They differ from each other in terms of the variables that influence them.
2. Many children with autism exhibit speech that does not change much. Variability is just like any other aspect of behavior. Its antecedents and consequences influence it. Variability can be increased through the following:
   (a) Simple reinforcement of novel behavior and by reinforcing verbal behavior that is different from the previous response and
   (b) Prompting novel responses and by using scripts and script fading to prompt novel verbal behavior.
3. Successful communication involves many more things than verbal behavior. These include the following:
   (a) Having an effective communication partner.
   (b) Using gestures, affect, and posture appropriate to the context of what is said.
4. Learning verbal behavior is a huge task. Do not underestimate the enormity of this task or fool yourself by thinking that you have made more progress than you really have.
5. Distinguish between form and function in verbal behavior. This is hard and elusive for even the best-trained people.
6. Your child will learn more if you recruit well-trained staff. Find BCBAs. If you cannot find BCBAs, then find people with real skill and professional training and commitment to teaching children with autism well.
7. Get educated about verbal behavior. Read online. Get some good books. Go to conferences. Network with other parents and professionals.

The Last, Last Word

Let me end by saying that there is no greater thrill than seeing a child with autism learn verbal behavior. It requires patience and skill—and it is worth it. When I think of the little boy who now says, "Excuse me!" instead of pushing someone out of the way, or a young woman with autism who asked me, ". . . and how are you?" I know it is all worthwhile. If you have a child with autism or you work with children with autism, persevere. It is hard work. It is also thrilling!

References

Note. Much of the research that is the basis for this book has been published in the *Journal of Applied Behavior Analysis.* You can search for articles at http://seab .envmed.rochester.edu/jaba/jabaindx.asp.

Dib, N., & Sturmey, P. (2007). Reducing student stereotypy by improving teachers' implementation of discrete trial teaching. *Journal of Applied Behavior Analysis, 40,* 339–343.

EnableMart (2008). *Edmark Reading Program (Print Edition).* Retrieved January 7, 2008 from www.enablemart.com/catalog/riverdeep/Edmark-Reading-Program-Print-Edition

Garcia, E., Baer, D. M., & Firestone, I. (1971). The development of generalized imitation within topographically determined boundaries. *Journal of Applied Behavior Analysis,* 4, 101–112.

Individuals With Disabilities Education Improvement Act of 2004, 20 U.S.C. § 1400 *et seq.* (2004) (reauthorization of IDEA 1990)

Lee, R., & Sturmey, P. (2006). The effects of lag schedules and preferred materials on variable responding in students with autism. *Journal of Autism and Developmental Disabilities,* 36, 421–428.

Lovaas, I. O. (1981). *Teaching developmentally disabled children: The me book.* Austin, TX: PRO-ED.

McClannahan, L., & Krant, P. (2005). Teaching conversation to children with autism: Scripts and script fading. Bethesda, MD: Woodbine House.

Partington, J. W., & Sundberg, M. L. (1998). *The assessment of basic language and learning skills* (ABLLS). Pleasant Hill, CA: Behavior Analysts.

Partington, J. W., & Sundberg, M. L. (2001). *Teaching language to children with autism or other developmental disabilities.* Pleasant Hill, CA: Behavior Analysts.

Poulson, C. L. (2008). Behavioral theory and language acquisition. In A. Fitzer & P. Sturmey (Eds.), *Language and autism spectrum disorders: Applied behavior analysis, evidence and practice.* Austin, TX: PRO-ED.

Pyramid Educational Consultants (2008). Home of PECS (The Picture Exchange Communication System) and the Pyramid Approach to Education. Retrieved January 7, 2008 from www.pecs.com

Sarakoff, R., & Sturmey, P. (2004). The effects of behavioral skills training on staff implementation of discrete trial teaching. *Journal of Applied Behavior Analysis,* 37, 535–538.

Skinner, B. F. (1957). *Verbal behavior.* New York: Appleton-Century-Crofts.

Based on what your child has been doing for the last two weeks, write down things that might be a reinforcer.

Child's Name: _____

Date: _____

Possible reinforcer	Examples
Foods, such as snacks and candies	
Drinks, such as sips of Coke	
Toys, such as dolls and trains	
Activities, such as jumping on a trampoline	
Places, such as a favorite chair	
People, such as a favorite teacher assistant	
Secondary reinforcers, such as points, money, tokens	
Items or topics he or she likes to obsess on	
Things he or she likes to avoid or quit, such as crowded places	
Anything else he or she likes	

List the five most probable reinforcers. (List the very best one first, then the second best, and so on.)

1.

2.

3.

4.

5.

Child's Name: _____

Date: _____

Time	Approach Verbal (V) Hands (H) Body (B)	Avoid Verbal (V) Hands (H) Body (B)	Object or person approached or avoided

Child's Name: _____

Date: _____

Item	Order selected

	B	C	D	E
A				
B				
C				
D				

Summary of choices

Item	Tally
A –	
B –	
C –	
D –	
E –	

Directions: Record the time in blocks of 1 minute in the left column. Record the number of vocalizations in each minute in the right column.

Child's Name: _____ Date: _____ Time: _____

Reinforcer(s) Used: _____

Time	Number of vocalizations
Total	

About the Editor and Author

Richard L. Simpson, PhD, is professor of special education at the University of Kansas. He currently directs several federally supported projects to prepare teachers and other leaders for careers with children and youth with autism spectrum disorders. Simpson has also worked as a teacher of students with disabilities, a psychologist, and an administrator of several programs for students with autism. He is the former editor of the journal *Focus on Autism and Other Developmental Disabilities* and the author of numerous books and articles on autism spectrum disorders.

Peter Sturmey, PhD, is a professor at Queens College, City University of New York, and a faculty member in the Learning Processes and Neuropsychology Programs of the Graduate Center, City University of New York. He is also affiliated with the doctoral internship in psychology program at Louisiana State University and Pinecrest Developmental Center and is an honorary senior lecturer at the GKT Dental Institute, Kings College, London. He has published several books, including *Functional Analysis in Clinical Psychology;* more than 100 peer-reviewed papers; and more than 25 book chapters related to applied behavior analysis and developmental disabilities. He is on the editorial board of several journals, including *Research in Developmental Disabilities, Journal of Positive Behavioral Interventions, Journal of Applied Research in Intellectual Disabilities, International Journal of Consultation and Therapy, Journal of Intellectual Disabilities Research,* and *Research in Autism Spectrum Disorders.*